Salmon, Ghosts, & Bugs

Suffering in the Wet Woods

Mark Huck

Contents

Dedication..9

Preface..11

Prologue 13

Chapter 1: Ghost Forests...........................17

    Tectonic Plates...20

    The Wet Woods 23

    The Orphan Tsunami 26

    The Boxing Day Tsunami............................29

    The Cycle of Chaos 30

Chapter 2: Salmon Runs...........................35

    Food chain..40

    Life cycle 47

    The Pacific migrations................................50

    Humans 51

    Running the Gauntlet.................................70

Chapter 3: Bugs 75

    Smallpox...78

Pandemic of 2020-21 82

Children in the summer of 2020 86

Chapter 4: The Problem of Suffering................................117

Polytheism 120

Dualism 122

Monotheism 123

Creator-only 132

Mass-extinction events 133

Food chains 134

Suffering, logic, and Creator 135

Defenses 140

Choice between evolution and two-faced Creator 141

Why humans need good and evil......................................143

Occam's razor 143

Chapter 5: So what? 145

Appendices 151

Appendix A: Getting there 152

Appendix B: Great salmon dinners 166

Appendix C: Footnotes 169

Dedication

This book is dedicated to the members of the U.S. Fisheries Service and their counterparts at state and local levels energetically helping salmon survive and flourish, and to the world's frontline health care workers putting their lives on the line so we may also see tomorrow.

Preface

Most of us love to light up the grill and plop a cedar plank – on which lay beautifully carved sections of a salmon – into the inferno. Not 15 minutes later, the most delectable fish is added to our feast.

We don't really think about it too much: how the salmon arrived on our plate. We concern ourselves with various rubs, dressings, and other additives to further enhance the protein that awaits.

God, or Nature, has put these doomed fish on the earth to nourish a vast number of species, land, air, and water bound: humans, seals, pelicans, whales, bears, eagles, and many, many more. And this all minute-by-minute for millions of years.

The accumulated debt of life to the salmon is immeasurable. Yet these poor creatures would, if not snatched from life, be sent starving up impassable rivers, enduring rocks and fallen trees, evading eager predators, only to spawn briefly and finally die, if they even get that far, which only one-in-thousands ever does.

It is a severe, perhaps unassailable, problem for a God claiming to be good or loving.

Spawn and die along Piper's Creek at Carkeek Park, Seattle

Prologue

We drove up the winding road into Seattle's Carkeek Park, terminus of the Carkeek Watershed, and parked. The park was serene. Quiet.

Our friends wanted to see the salmon going upstream, and Pipers Creek was a scant 3 miles from our house. Near some explanatory signs were a couple of park rangers. They answered many of our questions, most revolving around the number of eggs versus the number of survivors. We did not ask about God.

The scene all along the creek was carnage. It was difficult to tell if the salmon had reached a spawning point and renewed their treacherous, tortuous cycle, or had died in the attempt. Judging by the color of the fish, these were unsuccessful males. Decaying carcasses of the failed upstream attempt lined the stream. Eagles perched at the tops of trees, ready to assist the conclusion of the cycle.

We all were quickly disabused of the notion that salmon migrations – indeed, their entire lifecycle – was anything close to romantic. Rather, it was painful to watch, painful to understand, mainly depressing in its seeming futility. Yet, this very cycle had been going on continuously for tens of millions of years, far longer than the brief appearance (to date) of man.

What did this monstrous migration tell us about life? About anything that might have had a hand in its creation? I'm sure the jolt of watching the finale of the migration left our friends with similar questions. We didn't speak about it, though. We buried it deep. The questions burned.

But this wasn't the only massive natural phenomenon that spoke of incredible suffering over vast periods of time, belying notions of love and good.

Before the salmon was the water in which they swam, and the land masses moving below those oceans. While the salmon's suffering was annual and peculiar, the engulfing earthquakes occurring a few times each millennia meted out a more democratic disaster. When underwater, the quakes unleashed terrific walls of water that quickly crashed against the nearest shores, wiping out most of the life tenuously clinging there. It was total. Only the eventual rise of the land could halt the relentless wall.

There were the lucky creatures, however, that either were so small they simply rode out the disaster, those that dove deep for cover, or those that flew above. All else met the punishment.

Before turning attention to the salmon, these horrific consequences of the ever-cooling earth are the focus. What do these massively destructive and impersonal events tell us about any underlying Architect, the same who sends the salmon on their pain-riddled, deadly journeys?

Chapter 1: Ghost Forests

In 1986, geologist Brian Atwater slogged through the water of Washington's Neah Bay, pulling soil sample after sample out of the muck, attempting to confirm his hunch that massive earthquakes had continually rocked the Pacific Northwest, a history hinted at by Native American legends of great floods and upheavals. These myths had teased geophysicists: was this corner of the world seismically docile as many believed? Or, was it more akin to the earthquake-prone neighbors in Alaska and California? Atwater wondered whether the answers might be found in the region's coastal geology, matching his findings with other work in known subduction zones in Japan and Chile.[1]

A year later he came forth: a series of major earthquakes and resulting tsunamis had left behind their unmistakable signature in the coastal sedimentary record. His paper stunned his colleagues but its data were unassailable. Building upon Atwater's findings and using data from tree ring records from "ghost forests" destroyed by coastal submergence, scientist David Yamaguchi narrowed down the date of the most recent large Cascadian seismic event to the year 1700, roughly. But was there more evidence? What might provide a clue to the size of the earthquakes?

Tectonic Plates

The North American Plate is a tectonic plate covering most of North America, Cuba, the Bahamas, extreme northeastern Asia, and parts of Iceland and the Azores. With an area of 29 million square miles, it is the Earth's second largest tectonic plate, behind the Pacific Plate. Between these massive sections of earth crust lies the Juan de Fuca Plate, one of the earth's smallest plates. The rate of convergence between the Juan de Fuca Plate and the North American Plate is 2.4 inches per year.[2]

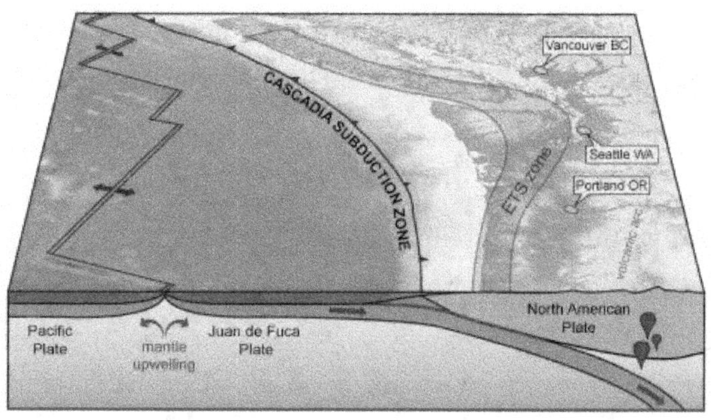

Graphic courtesy of US Geological Survey.

Where these plates collide off the Washington coast – the convection of the mantle driving the Juan de Fuca under the North American Plate[3] and generating nearly continuous earthquakes – is known as the Cascadia Fault.

However, as the plates attempt to slide past each other, they

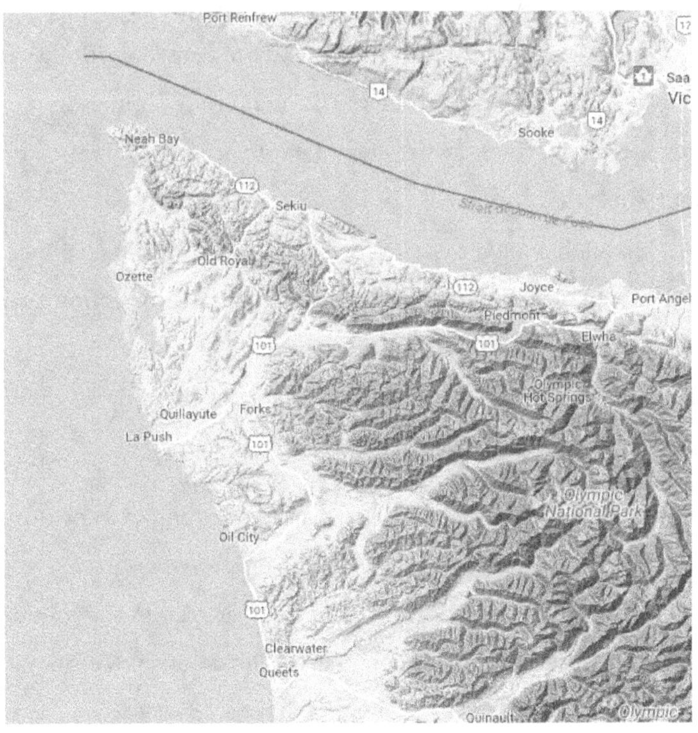

Olympic Mountains: crumpled tectonic plates

often get stuck, creating tremendous tension and a vertical uplift. We see this as the Olympic Mountains.

Subduction, then, is the story of the Pacific Northwest underfoot. For most of 200 million years this convergent boundary has been active and remains so: still producing earthquakes, and still raising mountains. It's called the Cascadia Subduction Zone.

Bits and pieces of continents and island arcs may randomly arrive at the subduction zone, mucking up the subduction process the way too many sheets of paper at once can muck up a paper-shredder. In the case of the Olympics, there was a mass of land north (Vancouver Island) and an accreted terrane to the south (the North Cascades), and a bend in the subduction zone itself. In essence, too much material is being stuffed into the subduction zone, so the excess material goes the only way it can: up.

As the plates slip by one another, a sudden twang of pent-up energy is released periodically, its tremor known as an earthquake. In geological time – time considered in the millions of years – these quakes happen nearly continuously. To humans with a much smaller time scale, they happen every 20 generations or so.

The twang also displaces massive quantities of the water above, and the Pacific Ocean sends a wave known as a tsunami crashing across the ocean in the two directions leading away from the fault. Heading east, the tsunami hits the Washington coast about 15 minutes after the twang, washing salt water over the landscape.

The Wet Woods

The crumpled mass of material known as the Olympic Mountains then forces the air from the Pacific up into ever cooler temperatures where that air condenses and, when too heavy, rains. The Pacific winds are constant and, accordingly, the rains are constant, feeding the enormous trees that have evolved on the Olympic Peninsula to take advantage of this constant watering. The trees tower to over 200', dwarfing the animal life below.

While animal life sees the trees and feels the rain, it has no visibility into the forces beneath the surface, unleashed at seemingly random intervals – by animal standards. Those animals on the coast would simply see the sea recede toward the horizon, followed minutes later by a massive, unavoidable wall of water destroying all before it.

Final beneficiary of the ascending Olympic Mountains: trees gathering in the constant fall of massive quantities of Pacific-sourced rain.

Human Settlement

About 15,000 years ago, as the last of the great Ice Ages ended, humans wandered across a land bridge that was disappearing between what are now Russia and Alaska. These people moved southeastward, hugging the coast to reap benefit of its fish and wildlife, slowly populating the coast all the way from North to South America. As they traveled, the 10-generation tsunamis would wipe out many of them, but the survivors would reproduce, and so the migration would recommence.

"In the oral traditions of Coast Salish cultures and other Pacific Northwest First Nations, Thunderbird and Killer Whale tales relate specifically and metaphorically to past catastrophic events even though they are presented in mythical scenarios. They speak of unspeakable things that once took place along the coastal corridor from northern California to southern B.C.

Forty times, to be exact, since the last glacial period, according to earth scientists. Nineteen of which were full rupture 9.0 megathrust earthquakes along the 1,000-kilometre Cascadia Subduction Zone, the last of which took place on Jan. 26, 1700 at 9 p.m."[4]

The Orphan Tsunami

Near midnight on January 27, 1700, a sudden tsunami inundated several villages on the eastern coast of Japan. No earthquake had proceeded it. It simply came.

The waves reached as high as 12 feet and flooded rice paddies, washed away buildings and damaged fishing shacks and salt kilns. Sleeping villagers awoke startled and wet and had to hastily scramble to high ground. The waters knocked down oil lamps and started a fire in one village and destroyed 20 houses in another.

The waves pounded the villages all through that night and into the late morning of the next day.

They swept through Miho, a village about 90 miles (140 kilometers) southwest of what is now Tokyo, about seven times. But in the days leading up to the 1700 tsunami, no earthquakes had been detected. Miho's leader wrote that such a thing was unheard of and wondered what to call the waves. "It is said that when an earthquake happens, something like large swells result, but there was no earthquake in either the village or nearby," he wrote.[5]

Over time, this event was referred to as the "orphan tsunami": its cause was elusive.

There was no record from the other side of the Pacific where a 9-magnitude Cascadia earthquake had just thrust a wall of water perhaps 40' high crashing over the Olympic coast, decimating the small fishing villages that peppered the coast line. These native people had little hope of survival. Those that might have survived the wall of water would have recovered to a landscape of destruction and death, many family members likely washed far inland and crushed by the debris swept up with them.

As the massive wave moved toward the coast, the land simultaneously dropped, giving the wave a permanent new home far inland. The salt water started killing the trees.

Professor Yamaguchi's finding of a 1700 inundation of the Pacific Northwest coast coincided with the orphan tsunami. Traveling to Japan to speak with Japanese scientists, Atwater confirmed that the magnitude 9 earthquake in Cascadia had washed over the Japanese coast.

Aftermath

On the North American coast, inland animals would have simply felt a tremor at their feet. Perhaps feeding at higher altitudes, some might be caught by an avalanche, but most would have simply looked around without knowing, perhaps panicking. But it ended within hours and all was still again.

A ghost forest of dead red cedars stands along the banks of the Copalis River in Washington State. The grove is one of the clues that led scientists to reassess their understanding of the potential size of earthquakes that can be generated in the Cascadia Subduction Zone off the Pacific Northwest Coast. Brian Atwater, 1997, United States Geological Survey

Some animals would likely venture back toward the lower elevations, particularly those interested in food from the sea. A bewildering scene would await them, with tons of forest debris washing ashore with each tide. But it would be eerily quiet.

Not all the sea water would wash back to the sea. The sinking land would capture a lot of it in newly formed lakes and marshes. At first, trees would seemingly be thriving in a new swamp. But, slowly, the salty water would bring death to those forests, and future generations would refer to them as the "ghost forests."

The Boxing Day Tsunami

On December 26, 2004, a rupture along the fault between the Burma Plate and the Indian Plate created an undersea megathrust earthquake that registered a magnitude of 9.1–9.3 Mw, reaching a Mercalli intensity up to IX in certain areas.

A series of massive tsunami waves grew up to 100 feet high as they heading inland. Communities along the surrounding coasts of the Indian Ocean were devastated, and the tsunamis killed an estimated 227,898 people in 14 countries, making it one of the deadliest natural disasters in recorded history.[6]

A 2,600-ton vessel, was flung some 2 km (1.2 mi) to 3 km (1.9 mi) inland during the Boxing Day Tsunami of 2004. Si Gam Acèh, Public domain, via Wikimedia Commons

The Cycle of Chaos

For humans, the propensity to live near the coasts – where navigation assists trade and food is plentiful – has its costs over the long cycles of destruction. Each cycle wipes out coastal villages, slow to repopulate until a few generations pass and enough time to push the memory of the last tsunami into legends, if anywhere.

The forces propelling the earth's plates are ever in motion, and the cycle is unabated. There is no human intervention possible, only preparation for a known, forthcoming disaster. The geological record reveals that "great earthquakes" (those with moment magnitude 8 or higher) occur in the Cascadia subduction zone about every 500 years on average, often accompanied by tsunamis. There is evidence of at least 13 events at intervals from about 300 to 900 years with an average of 570–590 years. Previous earthquakes are estimated to have been in 1310 AD, 810 AD, 400 AD, 170 BC and 600 BC.[7]

Recent findings conclude that the Cascadia subduction zone is more complex and volatile than previously believed. In 2010, geologists predicted a 37% chance of an M8.2+ event within 50 years, and a 10 to 15% chance that the entire Cascadia subduction zone will rupture with an M9+ event within the same time frame.[8]

"When the next very big earthquake hits, the northwest edge of the continent, from California to Canada and the continental shelf to the Cascades, will drop by as much as six feet and rebound thirty to a hundred feet to the west – losing, within minutes, all the elevation and compression it has gained over centuries. Some of that shift will take place beneath the ocean, displacing a colossal quantity of seawater. The water will surge upward into a huge hill, then promptly collapse. One side will rush west, toward Japan. The other side will rush east, in a 700-mile liquid wall that will reach the Northwest coast, on average, 15 minutes after the earthquake begins. By the time the

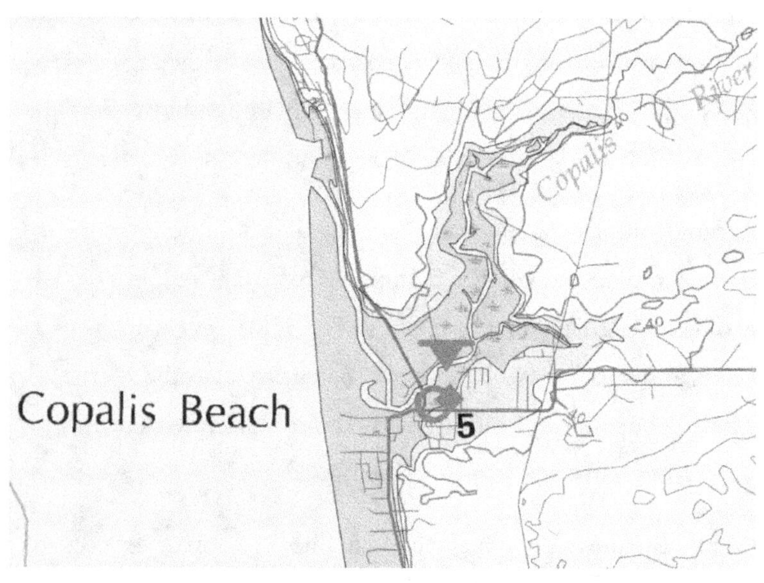

Inundation map of Copalis Beach. Washington Department of Natural Resources[9]

shaking has ceased and the tsunami has receded, the region will be unrecognizable."[10]

For Copalis Beach, Washington, the ghost forest there will again be inundated, the town destroyed. Newborns will join all life in this misery. It is difficult to reconcile with a God who is good. It is the force of nature arriving at random intervals in an animal's time horizon. No one is spared, unless luck is with that creature.

The ghost forests taunt us: where is love or goodness, or a God encompassing these virtues?

Salmon.

Chapter 2: Salmon Runs

The cycle of chaos brought on by the Cascadia Fault earthquakes occurs over centuries. For salmon, however, the cycle is every few years, for over (approximately) the most recent 1% of the earth's existence.

The Eocene Epoch began about 56 million years ago, and it is during this 20 million year period that salmon as we might recognize them appeared. Scientists have named this earliest but extinct predecessor of salmon *Eosalmo*. Fossils of this ancestor have been found in the State of Washington – at the Stonerose fossil site[11] nearly 200 miles from Puget Sound though 20 miles from the Columbia River – dated to 48 million years ago.

Eosalmo driftwoodensis, the oldest known salmon in the fossil record, helps scientists figure how the different species of salmon diverged from a common ancestor. The British Columbia salmon fossil provides evidence that the divergence between Pacific and Atlantic salmon had not yet occurred 40 million years ago. Both the fossil record and analysis of mitochondrial DNA suggest the divergence occurred 10 to 20 million years ago. This independent evidence from DNA analysis and the fossil record indicate that salmon divergence occurred long before the glaciers (of Quaternary glaciation) began their cycle of advance and retreat.[12]

A million years ago

Oncorhynchus nerka, a Pleistocene Sockeye Salmon, is from outcrops along the South Fork Skokomish River, Olympic Peninsula, Washington State. The fossils beds are abundant with large, 45–70 cm, four-year-old adult salmon[13]

A complex series of geologic events creating great reverses in the fresh and salt waters came with each arrival and departure of an Ice Age, starting with the Cordilleran Ice Sheet starting 2.6 million years ago.[14]

After the ice began melting and retreating north, the landscape slowly changed – both the land and sea levels rising – and great freshwater lakes forming in the lowlands filled with glacial waters from the melting ice. The sea levels rose quite considerably, almost an inch per year between 18,000 and 13,000 years ago. The isostatic rebound (rising) of the land rose even higher with an elevation gain of about four inches per year from 16,000 to 12,500 years ago. Around 14,900 years ago, sea-levels had risen to a point where the salty waters of Puget Sound began to slowly fill the lowlands.[15]

But salmon sit nearly atop the deadly competitive heap know as the food chain. Life clamors to get a leg up on the competition, leading to winners and losers. The losers generally play the numbers game, ensuring survival by creating thousands or millions of copies of themselves. Because salmon are not at the pinnacle, this is their genes' strategy as well.

Food chain

Why bring up the food chain? Because the fate of the salmon is not dissimilar to the fate of every step of the food chain, starting at the very bottom. Even the Sun is consumed, but by itself. Looking at the food chain gives us perspective on the salmon and, ultimately, ourselves.

Sun

The Sun is the initial source of energy on Earth. Yet, that energy is a byproduct, cast off into the universe as the Sun's unrelenting atomic fusion continues. The heat fuses about 600 million tons of hydrogen into helium every second, converting 4 million tons of matter into energy every second as a result. The Sun is dying.

Sunlight on the surface of Earth arrives at 1,000 watts per square meter in clear conditions when the Sun is near the zenith. A person weighing 100 kg who climbs a 10' ladder in 5 seconds is doing work at a rate of about 600 watts. The Sun provides a lot of energy.

Thus, the initial source of life resides in the death of the star at the center of our solar system.

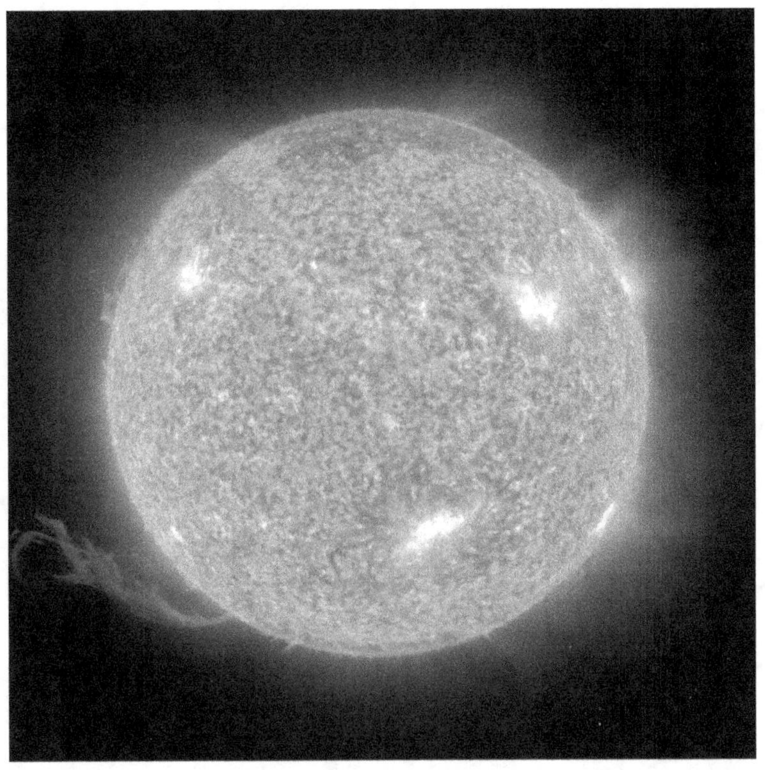

Physics.upenn.edu

Photosynthesis

One of the great evolutionary steps was harvesting the Sun's energy. Plants, algae, and some types of bacteria change the

Sun's light into biological energy through a process called photosynthesis.

During photosynthesis, plants take in carbon dioxide (CO_2) and water (H_2O) from the air and soil. Within the plant cell, the water is oxidized, meaning it loses electrons, while the carbon dioxide is reduced, meaning it gains electrons. This transforms the water into oxygen and the carbon dioxide into glucose. The plant then releases the oxygen back into the air, and stores energy within the glucose molecules.

Herbivores then obtain this energy (now glucose) by eating plants, and carnivores obtain it by eating herbivores.[16]

Phytoplankton, plants, and bacteria

Phytoplankton obtain their energy through photosynthesis, as do trees and other plants on land. This means phytoplankton must have light from the sun, so they live in the well-lit surface layers (euphotic zone) of oceans and lakes. In comparison with terrestrial plants, phytoplankton are distributed over a larger surface area, are exposed to less seasonal variation and have markedly faster turnover rates than trees (days versus decades). As a result, phytoplankton respond rapidly on a global scale to climate variations. Phytoplankton form the base of marine and freshwater food webs and are key players in the global carbon cycle. They account for about half of global photosynthetic activity and at least half of the oxygen production, despite amounting to only about 1% of the global plant biomass.[17]

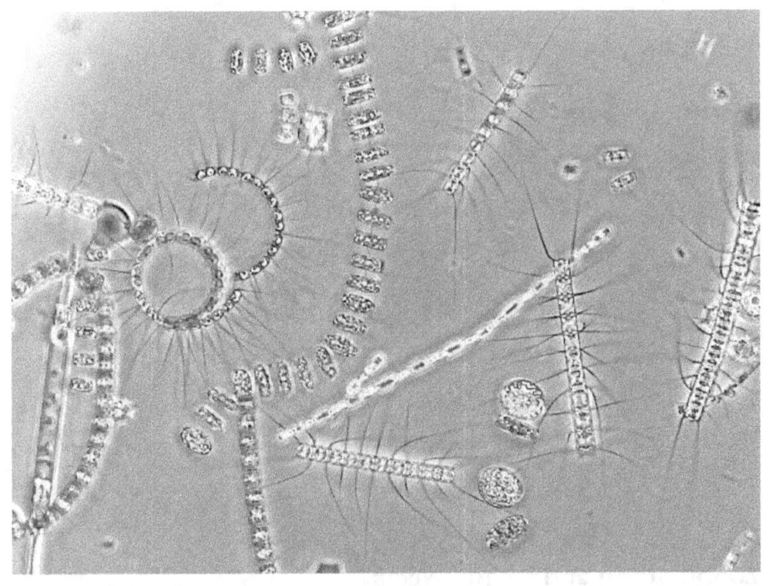

Phytoplankton. By NASA. Credits: University of Rhode Island/Stephanie Anderson. - NASA Earth Expeditions, Public Domain, https://commons.wikimedia.org/w/index.php?curid=95501788

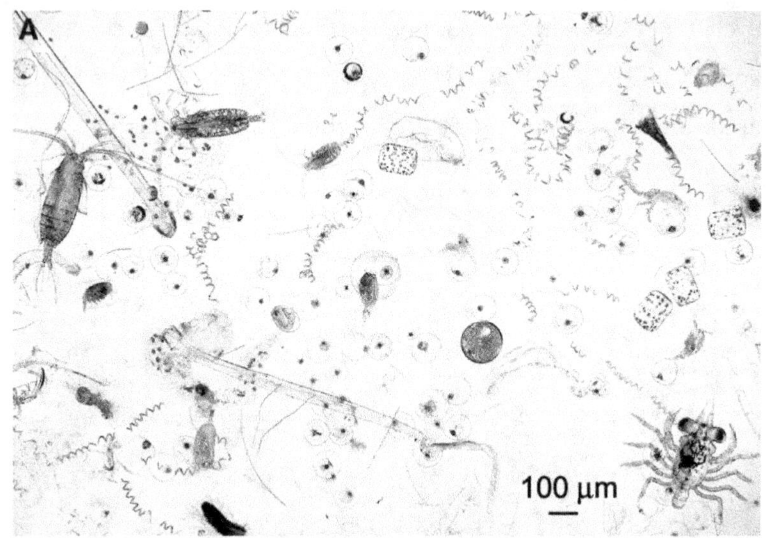

Plankton. By Jay Nadeau, Chris Lindensmith, Jody W. Deming, Vicente I. Fernandez, and Roman Stocker. Image courtesy of David Liittschwager. - Extracted from this Commons file, CC BY-SA 4.0, https://commons.wikimedia.org/w/index.php?curid=106438820

Zooplankton and small insects

Primarily by grazing on phytoplankton, zooplankton provide carbon to the planktic foodweb, either respiring it to provide metabolic energy, or upon death as biomass or detritus. Organic material tends to be denser than seawater, so it sinks into open ocean ecosystems away from the coastlines, transporting carbon along with it. This process, called the biological pump, is one reason that oceans constitute the largest carbon sink on Earth. However, it has been shown to be influenced by increments of temperature.[18]

Seaweed and bivalves

At the next layer, life starts to knock at the door of human diets as well as those of sea mammals. Oysters, mussels, kelp, and clams are predominant at this level.

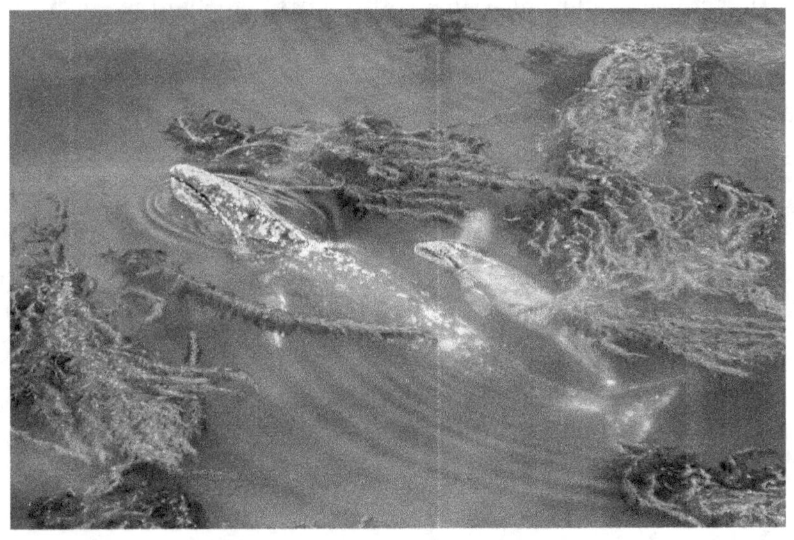

Whales in a kelp forest. Courtesy The Nature Conservancy.

Forage and herbivorous species

Squid, anchovies, sardines and other grazers occupy the next tranche, followed on top by carp, tilapia, and catfish. So far, the food chain is playing nice: this level gets their energy from plant or decaying life. Unfortunate for them, they are tasty to larger fish.

Predatory fish

Salmon and tuna are fishers of fish. The traditional meme of a larger fish swallowing a smaller fish starts here. But these fish must be looking over their fins: they are as hunted as they are hunting. For all sea life under the top tier, reproductive success is a numbers game: only one salmon in a thousand (at best) survive to reproduce again.

Seals, sharks, birds, bear, humans

Finally, however, the salmon become prey. Those animals at the top of the food chain are on the prowl for the densest protein sources at the least cost. Thus, the salmon transport the Sun's energy, in the form of dense protein, into the Wet Woods.

Life cycle

Although a single female salmon can lay 1,000 to 17,000 eggs, very few of those eggs actually survive from fertilization to maturity. An average of 3 fish returning for every parent fish that spawns would be considered good production. Many natural and human-related factors cause this high mortality. During spawning eggs may not be fertilized, or may not get buried in the gravel before they are either eaten by predators (birds and fish) or become damaged as they bounce along the river bottom. Some eggs may not mature and hatch due to freezing, drying out if the water level drops too low, being trapped in the gravel, or being smothered by silt.[19]

Those eggs that successfully hatch to "alevin" stage continue to grow, and then emerge from the gravel as "fry." Fry become subjected to a whole new batch of obstacles and predators, since salmon at this stage are near the bottom of the food chain. Pink and chum salmon juveniles head out to sea immediately. The other species may spend as many as two years in freshwater before they head out to sea. During times of these seaward migrations you can find corresponding concentrations of predators, such as beluga whales, arctic terns, gulls, and other fish species.

Spawning

Salmon reach sexual maturity at 2 to 8 years old. Different species mature at different rates. See below for information on the spawning of each of the five salmon species on Togiak Refuge. When the adult salmon are ready to spawn, after their long journey homeward, they select spawning sites with water flow through the gravel which will provide oxygen for their eggs and carry away carbon dioxide.

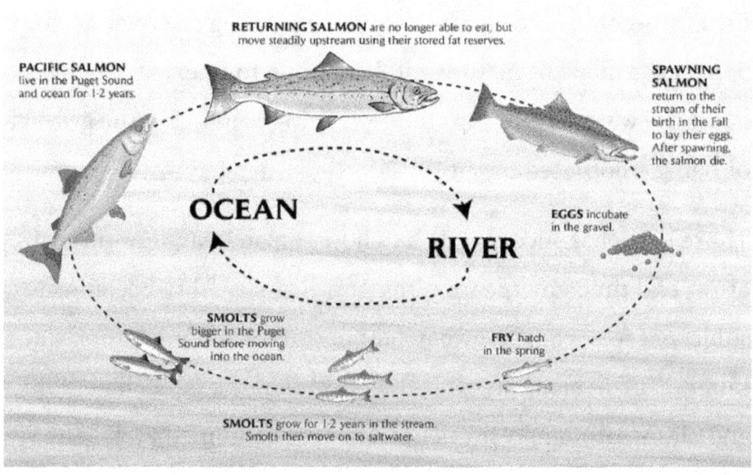

Once a female salmon selects a spawning site, she rapidly pumps her tail to wash out a depression in the stream gravel. After the eggs are laid, the female uses the same tail movements to completely cover the eggs with gravel. These gravel nests in which the salmon deposit their eggs are known as redds. Over several days, females may lay several more redds in a line upstream. A single spawning Chinook female can lay up to 17,000 eggs.

- Chinook: mature after 3-8 years; spawn July - August in large gravel and deep water with a strong current.
- Sockeye: mature after 4-5 years; spawn in August in fine gravel (2-7 cm in diameter) on lake shoals or slack water in rivers.
- Chum: mature after 3-5 years; spawn late July - August; spawn in gravel 2-3cm+ and upwelling currents in rivers or some shallow ponds or lakes.
- Pink: mature at 2 years; spawn August - September over coarse gravel and sand, in riffles with moderate to fast currents.
- Coho: mature at 4 years; spawn late September - December; utilize a wide range of spawning sites and currents, often in the farthest reaches of drainage.

The Pacific migrations

One of the most amazing facts about Pacific salmon is their ability to return to their "natal" or home stream or lake. Salmon are thought to use several navigation aids to find their way back to where they were hatched. Scientists believe salmon use a combination of a magnetic orientation, celestial orientation, the memory of their home stream's unique smell, and a circadian

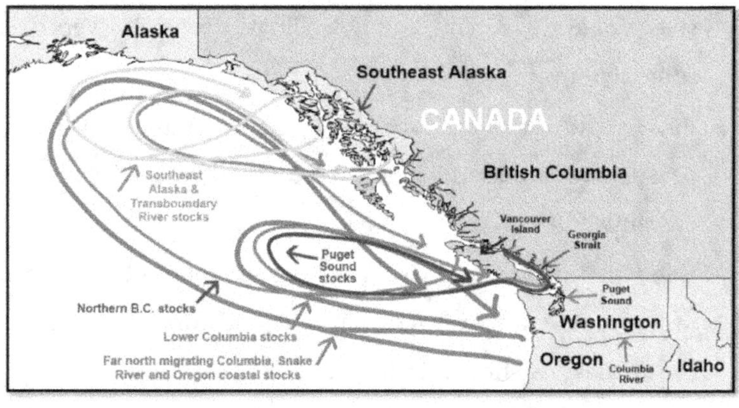

Many West Coast Chinook salmon stocks migrate far into the Pacific before returning to West Coast rivers as adults. Several of those returning stocks, such as those from the Columbia River system, overlap with the range of Southern Resident killer whales as they return to the Northwest. Graphic: NOAA Fisheries

calendar to return to their natal stream to spawn. The memory and smell centers in a salmon's brain grow rapidly just before it leaves its home stream for the sea. A salmon can detect one drop of water from its home stream mixed up in 250 gallons of sea water. Salmon will follow this faint scent trail, with the aid of the other methods mentioned above, back to their home stream to spawn.[20]

Humans

Compounding the risk of their food chain position, salmon now meet barriers hundreds of feet high and made of concrete.

Dams

A fully spanning dam on a river all but guarantees the end of a salmon run on that river. Salmon ladders, however, help bypass the blockage and allow some semblance of the migration. It would be difficult to determine whether the fish prefer a ladder or the old-fashioned rapids; they don't know. There are only obstacles.

"The hydropower dams have been controversial since before their completion, between 1962 and 1975, because of their disastrous impact on salmon and the other 137 species that are part of the salmon food chain. Most of the Columbia Basin's 250-plus dams have played roles in the salmon's decline, but the four lower Snake River dams are prime targets for removal because their economic value has diminished and their absence would inordinately benefit salmon.

"Even though the dams include ladders and other fish passage mechanisms, they have made salmon passage to and from the sea so difficult that populations have plummeted from already low mid-20th century levels. The dams effectively prevented all but a few salmon from carrying out some of nature's most astonishing migrations, reaching spawning grounds in Idaho's Snake River Basin as far as 900 river miles from the Pacific Coast and more than a mile in elevation. As a result, all three Snake River salmon species are endangered or threatened. Nevertheless, federal agencies and regional politicians have steadfastly declined to consider removing the Snake dams."[21]

Construction of the Ice Harbor Lock and Dam on the lower Snake River, photographed between 1956 to 1962. U.S. ARMY CORPS OF ENGINEERS

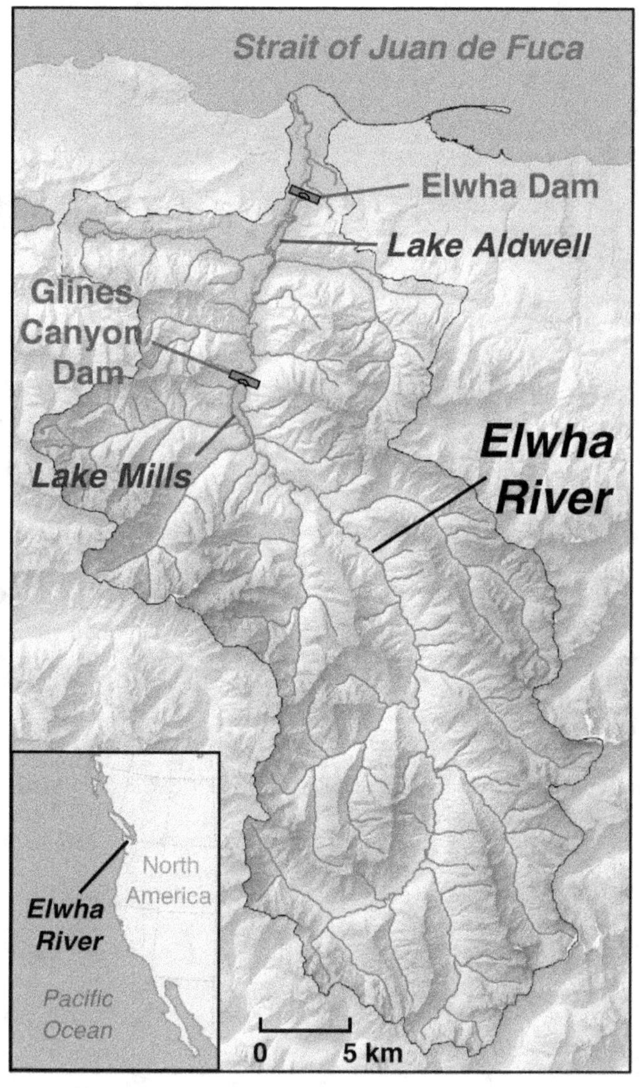

Courtesy USGS.

Elewah Dam removal

From 1911 to 2014, dams blocked fish passage on the lower Elwha River. Before the dams, 400,000 adult salmon returned yearly to spawn in 70 miles (110 km) of river habitat. Prior to dam removal, fewer than 4,000 salmon returned each year in only 4.9 miles (7.9 km) of habitat below the lower dam.[22]

Before: 2011. Photo by Ben Cody - Own work, CC BY-SA 3.0, https://commons.wikimedia.org/w/index.php?curid=16563772

The single biggest question surrounding Elwha Dam removal was: Would the fish return, after a hundred-year absence? Fish numbers have increased steadily since the dams came down, and by 2019 Elwha Chinook numbered well over 7,000 adults. Mike McHenry, fisheries biologist at the Lower Elwha Klallam Tribe, says that 2019 numbers suggest a fivefold increase for juvenile Chinook, the first "strong signal" for natural chinook production in newly available habitat.[23]

After: 2013. Photo by Zandcee - Own work, CC BY-SA 3.0, https://commons.wikimedia.org/w/index.php?curid=27438763

Fishing rights

Human competition for salmon often ends up in the courts, with indigenous tribes trying to enforce treaty provisions.

The Quinault Treaty was signed by Isaac Stevens, Governor of Washington Territory, and by Quinault Chief Taholah and other chiefs, subchiefs, and tribal delegates on the Quinault River on July 1, 1855 and at Olympia, on January 25, 1856. By the Treaty, the Quinault were immediately relieved of their lands while receiving only a vague promise of land in return:[24]

ARTICLE 1.

The said tribes and bands hereby cede, relinquish, and convey to the United States all their right, title, and interest in and to the lands and country occupied by them ...

ARTICLE 2.

There shall, however, be reserved, for the use and occupation of the tribes and bands aforesaid, a tract or tracts of land sufficient for their wants within the Territory of Washington, to be selected by the

President of the United States, and hereafter surveyed or located and set apart for their exclusive use, and no white man shall be permitted to reside thereon without permission of the tribe and of the superintendent of Indian affairs or Indian agent. And the said tribes and bands agree to remove to and settle upon the same within one year after the ratification of this treaty, or sooner if the means are furnished them. ...

ARTICLE 3.

The right of taking fish at all usual and accustomed grounds and stations is secured to said Indians in common with all citizens of the Territory, and of erecting temporary houses for the purpose of curing the same.

And so, for $25,000, the Quinault were penned in. However, the fishing rights continue to be embattled. In 2021, the Quinault sued to prevent commercial fishing at the river's estuary, those activities depleting their harvest just as one would suffocate another: cover the mouth.

Commercial fishing

Throughout the Northwest, harbors burst with fishing boats readying for the sea, the vessel sizes ranging from modest to huge ocean-going packing plants. While the commercial catches were endangered in the 1970s, they have recovered nearly 10-fold since then with the advent of government management.

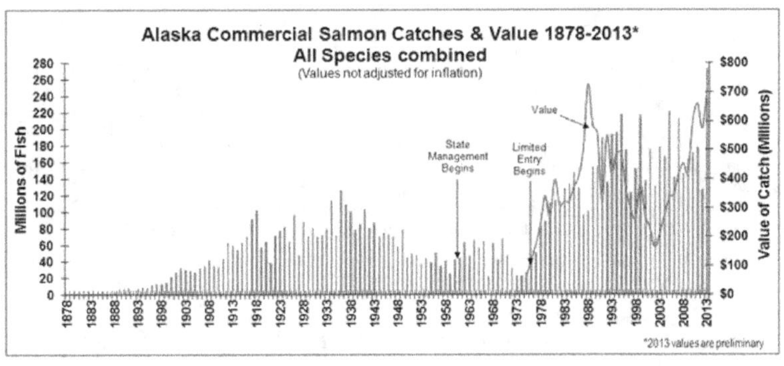

Alaskan salmon catch, 1878-2013.[25]

The stock is guarded during its seagoing phase by the North Pacific Anadromous Fish Commission which was established in 1992 to protect salmon beyond the 200 miles zones of its members: Japan, Korea, Russia, Canada and the USA. This itself was a followon from The Pacific Salmon Treaty of 1985 which formalised management between Canada and the USA of the fishing of salmon which crossed each country's shores on its way to the other's rivers.

The North American and Asian fishing efforts each make about half of the total catch although the majority of the more valuable species are caught by the Canadian and US fleets.

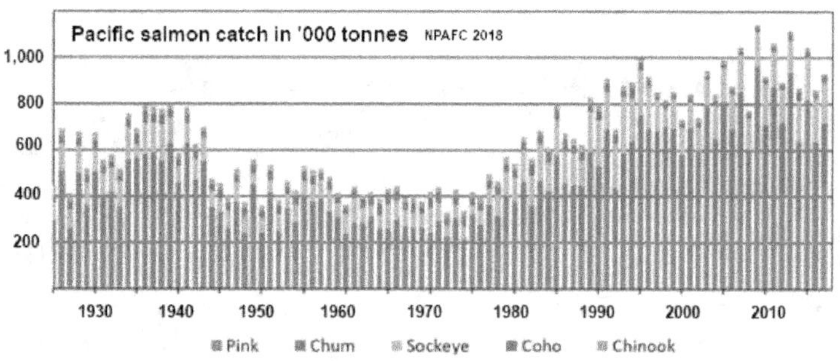

Pacific salmon catch.[26]

But this is not entirely the bounty of nature. Astonishing numbers of young salmon are released from hatcheries every year- three billion chum salmon, well over a billion pink salmon and 250 million each for chinook and sockeye. Hatcheries were first established in the late nineteenth century but they operated on only a small scale until the 1970s when the decline in the commercial catch suggested a bigger effort was needed. 700 million hatchery fish were released in 1968, 4 billion in 1982 and the figure since 1990 has stood at 5 billion a year. Ten hatchlings are released for every adult salmon caught. The rest keep other sea creatures well-fed.

The Seattle fleet readies for sailing.

In natural habitats the survival rate of wild salmon eggs to become "fry" – infant salmon about 4cms long - is about 10 per cent. Predation, bad weather, disease and shortage of food account for the rest. In a hatchery, however, over 90 per cent of eggs grow into fry. There are hundreds of hatcheries up Canadian and west coast US rivers and on the those of the eastern Pacific. The reason hatcheries focus on chum and pink salmon despite their being the less valuable species is that these two go to sea when they are just a few days or weeks old, whereas the other species need up to 18 months in freshwater, growing into much larger fish. As any hatchery has a fixed number of water tanks, it can produce many more pink and chum than other kinds.

At the Quinault National Fish Hatchery in Humptulips, Washington, over three million fish are managed, with about 660,000 Coho yearlings and 1.5 million Chum fry released each year.[27]

But the reverse side of the *catch* is the *run*. Large catches result in smaller runs. It is a zero-sum game. This problem is becoming critical on many rivers, as evidenced by the 2021 Yukon River Fishery Announcement revealing a drop of nearly 90% from the usual run size of 1,110,000 chum and coho salmon[28]. The impact on all parts of the food chain is drastic, leading many species to starvation. In this case, human activities are the culprit, from over-harvesting by commercial outfits to global warming.

The nearly 2,000-mile-long (3,200-kilometer) Yukon River starts in British Columbia and drains an area larger than Texas in both Canada and Alaska as it cuts through the lands of Athabascan, Yup'ik and other tribes. For these people, the dire problem is compounded by the escapement objectives to preserve the run for the next year. Only non-salmon catch is permitted to these people. This still does not help the local moose, caribou, and sea populations.

The average run in Alaska has dwindled for years, with a noticeable, persistent downslope by 2005. One wonders why the commercial catches weren't curtailed then or afterwards. The problem was evident.

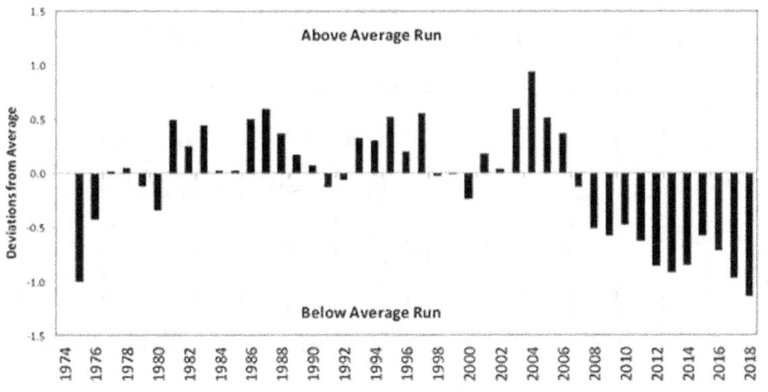

Alaska chinook runs[29]

Local scientists are pointing to global warming as the culprit. The Bering Sea, where the river meets the ocean, had unprecedented ice loss in recent years, and its water temperatures are rising. Those shifts are throwing off the timing of the plankton bloom and the distribution of small invertebrates that the fish eat, creating potential chaos in the food chain that's still being studied, said Kate Howard, a fisheries scientist with the Alaska Department of Fish and Game.[30] A department release in 2019 was already pointing to these issues[31]:

> Fluctuations in the survival of Chinook salmon smolt can significantly alter run strengths at local, regional, and statewide scales. For instance, the long-term marine survival for four Southeast stocks has been about four percent, meaning for every 100 smolt that emigrate to sea, four fish will return as adults over the next one to five years. Research has shown that during the recent period of poor production, marine survival has dipped below one percent. This decrease in marine survival, even in the face of some very good freshwater production in several systems, has been driving the downturn in overall adult production. The exact mechanisms

behind the increased mortality rates are unknown,
but environmental conditions such as precipitation,
air and ocean temperatures and water currents, to
name a few, are believed to affect juvenile salmon
survival.

While this crisis is reported as human suffering, the suffering of an entire species – Salmon – gets scant regard except as it impacts the top of the food chain.

Sport fishing

Adding further competition for the salmon's protein gift are private fishers.

"Meet at 3:15am at my porch," came the text message. My reply: "Oh dear." I traipsed over the Terry's place in the dark fully prepared for a Pacific squall.

The fog was dense and the night dark as Will drove the three of us to Westport. This was likely the most dangerous part of our fishing trip: unseen deer[32]. I was in the back seat. Will had the radio on, so I could hardly hear the conversation in the front, but managed to get bits and pieces to which I replied what likely were random comments. And so we made our way south along the coast.

We arrived in Westport at about 5am, having stopped a couple times to read signs that were barely visible through the fog. At the charter shop, we donned our masks and paid for our fishing licenses, then joined a dozen other folks on the "Sea Angel" and headed out to sea through the fog.

The Westport, Washington fishing fleet

The boat rolled with the sea as we made our way to some magical point in the middle of nowhere that the captain assured us was good fishing. Soon, birds appears, some floating in the water. They knew where the fish were. We were on track.

"Fish!" yelled the deckhand as the first bite yanked at someone's pole. He scampered to help, fish net in hand. As the salmon was reeled in, he snagged in in the net, pulled the hook out, then threw the fish on the deck, looking at the fins.

"It's wild," he pronounced with a dejected air, and threw the fish back in the ocean. We were only allowed to keep the hatchery fish, identifiable by an extra fin.

And so the morning went. The Pacific calmed to a glassy surface as we slowly reached our quota: two fish per person. It was a short morning; we'd found a good place to fish. The blue shark I caught was thrown back as well.

Back at the dock, a US agent checked the fish for tags, carefully recording those that had one to determine where it had originated. Then, we brought our fish back to the boat for filleting.

The catch.

With that, I had met a salmon run for the second time. This time, however, the salmon in our small catch was relieved of its duty to fight a river somewhere, then spawn and die. Once again, for perhaps a trillionth time, a salmon was going to provide protein up the food chain.

What, then, shall we eat?

Animal life is designed to live on a food chain. Protein must be obtained from somewhere on that chain. Moving further down the chain may be healthier, but it is not necessarily more morally defensible.

Even flipping over from carnivore to herbivore does not rid us of the fact that, when we eat, we are denying some life form its continued existence. Once growing, life is essentially life. Giving exalted status to one species is simply a byproduct of the human imagination. Slugs are precious. Insects fight for their survival.

Perhaps the best approach to determining a diet mix is to consider the impacts of one source of food on other life. If salmon stocks are dwindling, should I shift to vegetables to permit the stocks to replenish?

And so, this guide is not a call to boycott restaurants or sink fleets. Rather, it is a call to consume fellow life considerately. Take what's needed; harvest with as little pain to the prey as is possible.

A human population that requires only 2,000 calories per person per day impacts the food chain far less than one consuming 3,000 calories per person per day.

As well, environmental impacts can be managed with far greater awareness of impacts on life. This sensitivity has been heightened in recent years. Whether there is the political will to actually change large-scale and corporate behavior is another matter.

Running the Gauntlet

Not only are salmon squeezed in a eat-and-be-eaten food chain, their migratory route is damnable. Not only human but natural obstacles await their attempts to return home. River waters can be too low – hence, no passage over rocks – or too high – hence, too much flow to overcome. Trees can fall into the stream and block passage, as can avalanches. Bears prowl on the shores. Eagles hover high above. Is this "character building" for salmon? Of course not. There is no 'why', only 'is'.

Other species encounter similar seemingly insurmountable odds. Consider, for example, the sea turtle attempting to reach its first birthday a thousand mile down the Pacific coast, in Mexico.

The turtle eggs were deposited in the sand a few dozen feet from the unrelenting surf of the Pacific Ocean. In time, baby turtles no more than a couple inches in length emerge into the world of light and, as instinct will have it, head toward a surf 100-times their height.

This tsunami appears about every minute or less. It overwhelms the little creatures, sending them time and time again back onto the beach. Yet, again, they trample little by little toward the next wave, desperate to get beyond its undertow and into the early depths of the Pacific Ocean. With each rejection, the birds hovering far above sense a meal.

The female lays between 50-350 eggs in a "clutch", and may lay 1-8 clutches in a season. Thus, assuming turtles have not overcome the entire ecosystem and the females have 20 year of sexual maturity, only 1 in 20,000 of these baby turtles becomes a reproductive female. These are small odds, at best.

Humans watching the small turtles writhe toward the sea are

Heading into the tsunami. Sayulita, Mexico.

generally unaware of these out-sized odds. But the odds again bring up troubling questions about the force that set it all in motion, chief among the inquiries being, "do you care?"

Oh, and thanks for the love.

Plague Doctor, ca 1656.[33]

Chapter 3: Bugs

While the Pacific Northwest and its Wet Woods sit atop a massive geological fault and host many of the great salmon runs, the area is far removed from the large population centers where humans have historically passed bugs among themselves. The smallest of these bugs are known as viruses. But, these bugs care not for borders: they travel far and wide on the air currents, hoping to hitch a ride on the smallest of aerosols if the simple current does not suffice.

The bug presence in the Wet Woods reflects, therefore, the global dispersion of these pests, known to the human hosts as "the plague" or "a pandemic". While not as region-specific as tsunamis and salmon runs, they demand the same answers about the motive forces on Earth, for instance, "why?" and "do you care?"

Viruses are perhaps the most random form on the planet known as Earth. They are little more than a mathematical equation for reproduction, with the factors being air currents, temperature, available hosts, host precautions, other viruses, and so forth.

Viruses have no agency and no locomotion. They cannot decide to go somewhere. That decision is calculated by the air currents and host migrations. It is all calculated. There is no moral component to a virus: it is neither good nor bad. It simply is, and will follow the math laid before it.

Viruses are not life, if the elemental feature of life is the cell:[34]

> *A virus is a small collection of genetic code, either DNA or RNA, surrounded by a protein coat. A virus cannot replicate alone. Viruses must infect cells and use components of the host cell to make copies of themselves. Often, they kill the host cell in the process, and cause damage to the host organism.*

If life is good, viruses might play the bad guy. More likely, they both just *are*.

Smallpox

The virus behind smallpox is small, measuring approximately 300 nanometers by 250 nanometers[35], viewable only by an electron microscope. It spread in the air on a victim's cough. The last naturally occurring case of smallpox was diagnosed in October 1977. The risk of death after contracting the disease was about 30%, with higher rates among babies. Often those who survived had extensive scarring of their skin, and some were left blind.

In the 18th century, lucrative fur sales to China spurred an increase of trade in the Wet Wood – a/k/a Pacific Coast of the Olympic Peninsula – but the new traders brought infection. The first incidence of measles occurred in 1779. In the 1850's a series

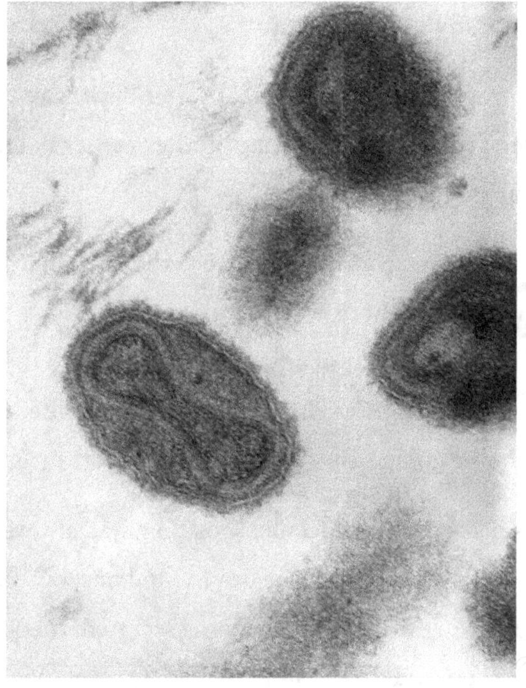

This transmission electron micrograph depicts a number of smallpox virions. The "dumbbell-shaped" structure inside the virion is the viral core, which contains the viral DNA; Mag. = ~370,000×[36]

of smallpox and influenza epidemics decimated the coastal population as they had done throughout North America the preceding two centuries. Too weak to resist the advance of white settlers and eager to preserve control of the Quinault River, the Quinault, along with the Queets, Quileutes, and Hohs, signedthe Quinault River Treaty in 1855, which established the Quinault Indian Reservation.

An early European explorer in Shoal-water Bay recounts the experience of the native Americans in the year 1852 at a place called Stony Point[37]:

> The place was considered sacred, and no Indian ever ventured there. Their usual superstitious reverence, and fear of any thing belonging to the 'memelose tillicums,' or dead people, prevented their ever going near the spot. ...

> This place, from its peculiar position, had always been a favorite residence with the Indians; but the chief having died, the village was secreted, the houses burned down, and the whole grown over with rose-bushes ...

... the Indians were afraid to go back there to live
on account of the dead people; but if a white man
went there they would go back too. ...

There is ... no disputing the face that an immense
mortality has occurred among these people, and
they are now reduced to a mere handful.

And so, in the tradition of the tsunami, the coastal people of the
Pacific Northwest were decimated. By the time of the Quinault
Treaty of 1855-56, the native people were ripe for exploiting.
What had they done to deserve this?

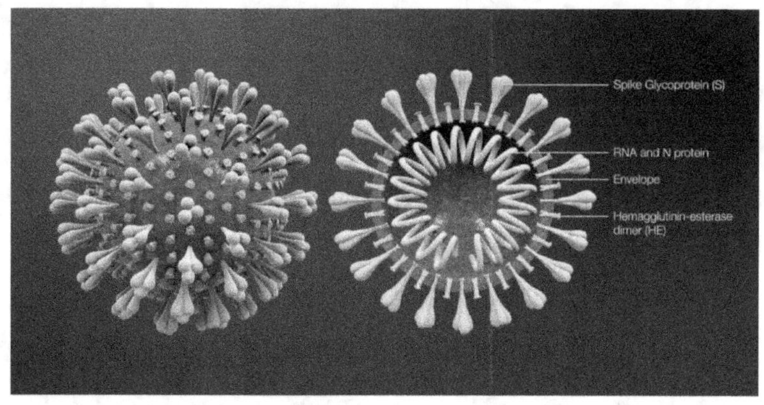

The coronavirus.[38]

Pandemic of 2020-21

The first case of Covid-19 in the U.S. arrived at Seattle's SeaTac airport on January 15, 2020. On January 21, the case is identified. Washington governor Jay Inslee signed a statewide stay-at-home proclamation and ordered to close non-essential businesses effective March 25 for two weeks, and so the Pacific Northwest human population shut down most social and business interactions.

By mid-April 2020, Grays Harbor County in Washington – the county encircling the Quinault Nation – had recorded only 3 cases of a new coronavirus that had been identified as the culprit for a disease known as Covid-19 in January of that year.[39]

But, by mid-September, that number had jumped to nearly 100, most of the increase in the previous month.[40] The daily rate of new cases holds at 10-15 per day through the end of November.[41]

Ten months later, average cases per day had increased to 71 as the cases per 100,000 reached 95: Grays Harbor was a hot spot.[42] Cases had reached 1 in 10 while deaths were 1 in 676.

The virus, as expected, had spread according to its mathematical certainty, aided by many hosts who refused masks and, later, vaccinations. Only half the Grays Harbor population had been vaccinated despite the vaccination's widespread availability.[43]

The impact on the limited capabilities of rural hospitals such as those in Grays Harbor only exacerbate the misery. Most of the patients showing up at the hospital in late 2021 were unvaccinated: they had the choice to prevent infection but chose instead to take up scarce resources at a local hospital. Other serious needs were put on hold.

This squeeze on resources results in triage: some needy cases simply get prioritized to the bottom of the heap. The lower the

7 Day Avg. of Bed Occupancy

Date	All hospital beds	Adult inpatient beds		ICU Beds	
Sept. 17, 2021	57.4	**99.7%**	36.3 of 36.4 beds used	**100.0%**	4.6 of 4.6 beds used
Sept. 10, 2021	62.7	**100.0%**	42.1 of 42.1 beds used	**100.0%**	5.6 of 5.6 beds used
Sept. 3, 2021	62.8	**97.6%**	40.8 of 41.8 beds used	**100.0%**	6.4 of 6.4 beds used
Aug. 27, 2021	59.7	**98.2%**	38.0 of 38.7 beds used	**86.8%**	4.6 of 5.3 beds used
Aug. 20, 2021	64.4	**99.3%**	43.1 of 43.4 beds used	**94.4%**	5.1 of 5.4 beds used
Aug. 13, 2021	60.9	**95.2%**	38.0 of 39.9 beds used		N/A
Aug. 6, 2021	63.0	**92.1%**	38.7 of 42.0 beds used		N/A
July 30, 2021	63.3	**99.3%**	42.0 of 42.3 beds used		N/A
July 23, 2021	60.2	**93.9%**	36.8 of 39.2 beds used	78.8%	5.2 of 6.6 beds used
July 16, 2021	60.0	**87.2%**	34.0 of 39.0 beds used	74.6%	4.4 of 5.9 beds used

Gray's Harbor County Hospital ICU availability in Fall, 2021[44]

probability of a "beneficial" result – usually determined on the ground at the hospital emergency room – the less likely ICU capacity will be consumed.

Thus, the notion of "excess deaths," generally about 50% higher than the Covid-19 deaths reported.

Country	Excess COVID-19 deaths	Reported COVID-19 deaths
United States of America	912,345	578,555
India	736,811	248,016

Excess deaths, March 2020 to May, 2021[45]

In retrospect it was an avoidable disaster. Before the pandemic washed ashore on U.S. beaches, other countries grappled with it and there were earlier epidemics; these guideposts were ignored. As we learned for ourselves in the moment, even our own guideposts were ignored, then mocked.

The fault lay not only with the nation's leadership, but also with its people. Science and scientists were the guiding star, and the only star. Only scientists could map and interpret the virus' path. Leaders and the led all too often ignored that light.

The unparalleled economic and personal pain of 2020 was avoidable. The U.S. had the opportunity to flex its medical, economic, and social muscle to bump the virus back into the ocean. We didn't. Instead, our leaders flailed and our people griped. It was as though all the learning that had occurred from

1918 onwards to the ever-moving present was forgotten. To be sure, there were many in the medical community who screamed about the dangers. These were screams in a vacuum.[46]

By 2021, the U.S. citizenry have at least a modicum of control over the result, with the wide availability of a vaccine in place from the beginning of 2021. In other words, the anti-vaxxers kept this human-centric pandemic in play far into 2021.

While humans have the advantage of not being proactively slaughtered to prevent transmission, animal herds are simply wiped out by their owners. For example, the foot-and-mouth disease in Taiwan during 1997 resulted in 3.8 million pigs being slaughtered, while 6 million sheep and cattle were killed in the United Kingdom in 2001 for the same reason.[47] The one million or so human victims of Covid-19 pale by comparison. Nonetheless, we own the presses.

Children in the summer of 2020

Adults simply ignored the dangers to their children during the Pandemic. As reported in the CDC's Morbidity and Mortality Weekly report on July 31, 2020, an early stage in the Pandemic[48]:

During June 17–20, an overnight camp in Georgia (camp A) held orientation for 138 trainees and 120 staff members; staff members remained for the first camp session, scheduled during June 21–27, and were joined by 363 campers and three senior staff members on June 21. Camp A adhered to the measures in Georgia's Executive Order* that allowed overnight camps to operate beginning on May 31, including requiring all trainees, staff members, and campers to provide documentation of a negative viral SARS-CoV-2 test ≤12 days before arriving. Camp A adopted most† components of CDC's Suggestions for Youth and Summer Camps§ to minimize the risk for SARS-CoV-2 introduction and transmission.

They found

SARS-CoV-2 spread efficiently in a youth-centric overnight setting, resulting in high attack rates among persons in all age groups, despite efforts by camp officials to implement most recommended strategies to prevent transmission. Asymptomatic infection was common and potentially contributed to undetected transmission, as has been previously reported. This investigation adds to the body of evidence demonstrating that children of all ages are susceptible to SARS-CoV-2 infection and, contrary to early reports, might play an important role in transmission. The multiple measures adopted by the camp were not sufficient to prevent an outbreak in the context of substantial community transmission.

Not only are young people potential carriers, they are hard-wired by their genes to engage in social activity regardless of many dangers.

On August 3, 2020, the 30,000-student Paulding School District in suburban Atlanta started classes. A picture of the hallway at North Paulding High School went viral on Twitter, with the photographer estimating a 10% mask rate[49]:

A week later, The Wall Street Journal (news department, to be sure) came out with a strong stance on school openings in the U.S. In an article entitled "Latest Research Points to Children Carrying, Transmitting Coronavirus" the Journal reported[50]:

Some schools in the U.S. can likely safely reopen, researchers say, but the new findings suggest the

facilities should proceed carefully. And, they added, schools should wait until community transmission is under control. They also should take steps that can reduce the risks for students and staff, such as widespread masking and frequent cleaning, along with social distancing and good ventilation, experts recommend.

A number of schools overseas have reopened with little incident after taking stringent precautionary steps. Without such actions, researchers warn, schools reopening in the U.S. could experience outbreaks like those that hit facilities in Israel and France.

"Our schools are little mini microcosms of our cities that they're in—what's happening in cities is what's going to happen in schools," said Tina Hartert, a professor of medicine at the Vanderbilt University School of Medicine, who is leading a study, funded by the National Institute of Allergy and Infectious Diseases, exploring the infection rate in children and people they live with across nearly 2,000 households in the U.S.

"Until there is definitive data one way or the other, we have reason to believe from decades of data from other respiratory viruses that children are very good transmitters," Dr. Hartert said. "There isn't a lot of reason to believe that that wouldn't be the case with this virus."

Several factors contributed to the initial thinking that children were less affected by Covid-19. The virus might not have spread among many children during the early months, in part because schools were closed, playgrounds were locked up and kids were at home. ...

"Our estimates of [how kids] spread the virus may have been a bit inaccurate earlier on," Children's

National Hospital's Dr. Simpson said. "And as
certain states have loosened restrictions and kids
have been able to congregate, it's showing that it
does spread, and we do have to factor in the
prevalence of the virus in the pediatric population."

She and a team of researchers published a study this
month in the journal Pediatrics finding a nearly 21%
positive Covid-19 test rate among 1,000 children and
young adults with mild symptoms who were tested
at an exclusively pediatric testing site this spring.

As is not unusual, the Wall Street Journal's editorial department
rebutted its news department. It the same issue, the editorial
department let loose a commentary piece entitled, "School
Closures Damage the Youngest Children," which focused on the
immediate threat to the child over against the spread via the
child to the community[51]:

Studies are showing that young children are
probably the least likely to contract Covid-19. When
they do, the virus poses minimal health risks. So far,
exactly 10 American children ages 1 to 4 have died
from it. Young children also aren't major spreaders
of the virus. Even for older schoolchildren, the
American Association of Pediatricians, the National

> Academies of Science, Engineering and Medicine,
> and the Centers for Disease Control and Prevention
> have recommended that schools reopen, noting the
> social, emotional, behavioral and academic harm of
> remaining closed.

Not sure how many children would prefer an uninterrupted education to a living parent. Does the author of this commentary or the WSJ care about creating orphans and all that does for child development? It's this incredibly myopic view of the nature of a virus that played out in the coming months.

A couple days later, North Paulding High School went online "after revealing that a half-dozen students and three staffers were diagnosed with COVID-19. The district said it needs time to disinfect the North Paulding High School building and look for other potentially infected individuals."[52]

> Angie Franks said both her nephews who attend the
> school have tested positive for COVID-19. One
> came home from school Monday unable to smell,
> she said in an interview with The Atlanta Journal-
> Constitution. His mother took him for testing and
> got results the next day that showed he had been
> infected with the coronavirus, Franks said. By then,
> his brother was exhibiting symptoms and was also

tested. His positive results were returned Wednesday.

The students are quarantining at home, but both went to North Paulding High on the first day of school last Monday. Franks said the boys' father notified the school on Tuesday and Wednesday after getting their test results.

"They sat in class all day long with no masks and not social distancing," Franks said. "And I have no idea how many kids they came into contact with."

She said the boys did not grasp the gravity of the virus and weren't encouraged to wear masks in classrooms or hallways by the school. Paulding County's school system is not mandating masks for students and staff, although it is supplying them for teachers.

Concerns about Paulding's safety planning led one school nurse to resign from the district last month.

What exactly would be the point of teachers wearing masks, but not students or staff, particularly in a crowded indoor space?

Some argued that the experience of schools during the 1918 Influenza Pandemic – cities that kept their schools open seemed to fare no worse and sometimes better than cities that closed school – meant that we'd be fine opening them this time around.

The 1918 experience was studied by a group of professors at the Center for the History of Medicine at the University of Michigan back in 2010. They noted two important differences that might make the analogy inappropriate. First, the housing conditions for U.S. families is much improved from 1918[53]:

> As influenza struck New York, the public school system encompassed nearly a million children, of whom 75% lived in tenements whose crowded and unsanitary conditions were notorious for promoting infectious diseases. For students from the tenement districts, school offered a clean, well-ventilated environment where teachers, nurses, and doctors already practiced—and documented—thorough, routine medical inspections.

The second was an early version of contact tracing: school officials were allowed to inspect the living conditions of the children[54]:

> [T]he success of school nurses in conducting medical school inspections in the fall of 1918 in part reflected their broader job portfolio in the early 20th century, which involved surveying the health

conditions of students and their families in their own homes, a task that is more problematic today due to legal considerations related to personal privacy, not to mention shrinking revenues for public health nursing.

The professors went on to conclude[55]:

> The perceived need for school hygiene has diminished over the past 90 years, due to a combination of laudable advances in medicine and health, complacency toward the threat of infectious diseases, and reticence among public officials to implement public health measures that could be interpreted as violating individual rights. Nevertheless, many health officials recognize the need to address this problem, even in a climate of diminishing public revenue, and have participated in studies and programs to expand health services in the schools, particularly for immigrant and underserved communities.38 Most experts agree that while staffing levels for school nurses leave room for improvement, the mechanism to uncover more common contagious diseases in the classroom is in place, though dispersed across a broader band

of health personnel and educators. The effectiveness of this process will be the subject of much debate as the novel 2009 H1N1 influenza pandemic unfolds.

By August 11, 2020, Paulding County had spiked to 50 new cases from an average of 30 the previous 5 days.[56] In Georgia's Cherokee County, 925 students and staff were quarantined after an August 3 opening.[57] That same day, Cherokee County published data that 1,130 students and 38 staff from more than a dozen schools were under a 2-week quarantine. 70 cases were confirmed in the schools, with many of the cases coming out of Etowah High School[58] where in-person instruction was postponed until August 31:

> "This decision was not made lightly," the school district said in a statement Tuesday. "As of this morning, the number of positive cases at the school had increased to a total of 14, with tests for another 15 students pending; and, as a result of the confirmed cases, 294 students and staff are under quarantine and, should the pending tests prove positive, that total would increase dramatically."

Adults have made children a test case. That the students and teachers were put up to this by the citizens they served was lamentable.

Etowah High School, Georgia, opens with no masks.[59]

The New York Times reported on the reopening fiasco[60]:

> Their experience reveals the perils of returning to classrooms in places where the coronavirus has hardly been tamed. Students and teachers have immediately tested positive, sending others into two-week quarantines and creating whiplash for schools that were eager to open, only to consider closing again right away.
>
> All of this has only further divided communities where parents and teachers have passionately disagreed over the safety of reopening.
>
> Depending on whom you ask, the string of positive tests and isolation orders in Cherokee County either proved the district's folly for opening schools during the worst American public health crisis in decades, or demonstrated a courageous effort to return to normal.
>
> "This is exactly what we expected to happen," said Allison Webb, 44, who quit her job as a Spanish and French teacher in the district because of her concerns about reopening schools, and who put her

daughter, a senior, in the district's remote-learning program. "It's not safe" to return to the classrooms now, Ms. Webb said.

But to Jenny Beth Martin, who wanted schools to reopen — even appealing directly to President Trump in a visit to the White House — the district's return has been a rousing success.

"I think that the opening plan is working," said Ms. Martin, a district parent and co-founder of the national Tea Party Patriots, a conservative political group. "They're checking, they're making sure when people have tested positive that they're watching the exposure and spread."

The experiment began and failed, but no matter. It was not the last story, and proved typical. To wit: Florida[61].

Gov. Ron Desantis (R-FL)—along with senior officials in the state's Department of Education—continue to press counties to reopen schools fully for the fall semester, including those experiencing significant upticks in coronavirus cases. DeSantis, a close ally of President Donald Trump, has been viewed inside the top echelons of the administration, including within the president's coronavirus task force, as leading the way on the school reopening issue. On several private phone calls with the nation's governors, Vice President Mike Pence has praised DeSantis for his work in containing the virus and flattening the curve, even as cases and deaths have piled up in the state. Dr. Deborah Birx, the task force coordinator, too, has highlighted DeSantis' efforts in recent weeks to stop the spread.

But on Monday, Florida recorded a record number of coronavirus-related hospitalizations—as well as record COVID-19-related deaths on Tuesday. And the total number of cases in children under the age of 17 has increased by 137 percent in the last four weeks.

Against such a disturbing epidemiological backdrop, state mandates to reopen schools have been viewed by some officials in counties such as Hendry and Hillsborough County as too restrictive—and have forced administrators such as Puletti to roll the dice.

"I made the choice because I didn't want to risk losing funding for this district," Puletti, who is set to retire in November, told The Daily Beast. "It's all very stressful."

The decision to reopen schools in Hendry County, announced during the board meeting Tuesday morning by Puletti, came after the superintendent spoke with senior officials in the state Department of Education over the weekend. Puletti told The Daily Beast that following a school board meeting August 4, in which members voted to extend virtual learning until further notice, he called the department "immediately" to inform the state about the decision. The state was not willing to allow the county to delay in-person learning, Puletti said, even with the increasing case numbers in the county.

By mid-August, 2020, the Atlanta Constitution was reporting the "number of students and teachers placed under quarantine for COVID-19 this week in the Cherokee County School District doubled from last week, with the number of new infections nearly tripling."[62] Adding:

As this second week of school comes to a close, the district is reporting 80 new confirmed cases of the coronavirus and 1,106 students and employees quarantined as a result. Last week ended with 28 cases and 563 under quarantine in the district of about 40,000 students.

The number of newly infected students more than tripled, to 66 from 20. Five staffers tested positive this week compared with one last week, and nine teachers compared with seven last week.

Most of the infected students were in high school, their numbers rising to 47 from 13 at the end of last week. Eleven elementary school students and eight middle school students tested positive this week.

All six high schools were reporting new cases.

Etowah and Woodstock high schools have closed due to their outbreaks, with each reporting 13 newly infected students this week causing 170 and 249 students to be under quarantine respectively.

Etowah became a national focus last week after a photograph showing scores of seniors huddled together without masks for a back-to-school moment went viral online. However, no senior there reported an infection last week and just two of the newly infected this week were seniors, according to the district's list.

Two Etowah High English teachers tested positive for COVID-19 last week, as did one this week, along with a teacher described as "digital."

Cherokee High had a dozen students reporting infections and 125 placed under quarantine this week but has remained open. So has Creekview High with seven new student infections and 161 students placed under quarantine this week.

River Ridge and Sequoyah high schools had one new student infected apiece this week, with two dozen students placed under quarantine this week at the first school and 30 at the latter.

Most of these schools enrolled about 2,000 students last year, though Cherokee High reported about 2,700 and Etowah High was close behind with 2,400. About 1 in 4 students countywide choose online learning to begin the school year.

Meanwhile, even the White House coronavirus task force found Georgia in trouble, saying[63]:

Georgia wasn't doing enough the curb the spread of COVID-19, but that report was not made public until Thursday when it was published by The Atlanta Journal-Constitution.

The document, which scrutinized data from Aug. 1 to Aug. 7, said that though new case counts were slightly down compared to the week before, Georgia still was experiencing "widespread and expanding community viral spread." And the state's rate of case increase of 213 per 100,000 that week remained about twice the national average.

The task force continues to place Georgia in the "red zone," meaning weekly reported cases are above 100 per 100,000 people and a positive test result greater than 10% for the population. 109 counties and 34 metro areas in Georgia — including Albany, Athens, Atlanta, Columbus, Gainesville, Macon, Savannah and Valdosta — meet that definition.

But teachers were seeing the threat to both themselves and their students. An Arizona school district was forced to cancel the start of classes due to a teacher sick-out[64]:

Two East Valley school districts voted to return to in-person classes on Monday, but one of them has been forced to reverse course after pushback from staff.

The Queen Creek Unified School District and adjacent J. O. Combs Unified School District voted earlier this week to reopen schools for in-person learning.

But on Friday afternoon, J. O. Combs announced that it would not open at all on Monday because too many teachers refused to show up.

Superintendent Gregory A. Wyman in a statement said the district had received an "overwhelming response" from staff indicating that they did not feel safe returning to classrooms with students.

Wyman said the district had received a high volume of staff absences for Monday, with teachers citing health and safety concerns.

"Due to these insufficient staffing levels, schools will not be able to re-open on Monday as planned," Wyman wrote. "At this time, we do not know the duration of these staff absences, and cannot yet confirm when in-person instruction may resume."

Teachers in Arizona let their feelings be known in a "Motor March" on July 22.

Colleges and universities, however, were less inclined to nix tuition dollars. Many of those institutions on the semester system were opening in August.

Eric Fink ✔
@EricMillerFink

Some #Tucson teachers with a message for @dougducey, @Supt_Hoffman and education leaders. @KVOA

4:43 PM · Jul 22, 2020 · Twitter for iPhone

Arizona Motor March by Teachers July 22, 2020[65], a shot over the bow of inept leadership.

The plight of the children reached down to even younger ages. Also in August, a Centers for Disease Control report on childcare was released. The report, entitled "Limited Secondary Transmission of SARS-CoV-2 in Child Care Programs — Rhode Island, June 1–July 31, 2020", found:

> Cases occurred in 29 child care programs, 20 (69%) of which had a single case with no apparent secondary transmission. Five (15%) programs had two to five cases; however, RIDOH excluded child care–related transmission because of the timing of symptom onset. In late June, a child aged 2 years attended child care for 6 days while potentially infectious, including 3 days before symptom onset (parent-reported fever to 100.3°F [37.9°C] and chills) and 3 days after symptom resolution. Ten of 11 child care contacts were tested for SARS-CoV-2 a median of 2 days after last exposure (range = 1–3 days); none had a positive test result. Epidemiologic investigation by RIDOH indicated adherence to RIDHS regulations.

> ***Secondary transmission in four child care***
> ***programs after July 15 could not be ruled out***.
> [Emphasis supplied]

So, in a 2-month period, 4 of 29 centers, 13.8%, might have had secondary transmission. In just 2 months. What about over the course of a year? Yet, at least two very prominent media reported that the CDC report indicated an "all clear". Absolutely not.

In a reversal, Florida thought about its children and teachers[66]: A Florida judge ruled on August 24, 2020, that the state's requirement that public schools open their classrooms for in-person instruction violated the Florida constitution because it "arbitrarily disregards safety" and denied local school boards the ability to decide when students can safely return.

By the end of August, more schools reported large number of infections among children at schools as the schools opened. Florida, which reopened its schools starting August 10, was particularly hard hit[67]:

> As schools begin to reopen in Florida, the state
> has confirmed that nearly 9,000 children had
> contracted COVID-19 over a 15-day period in
> August, according to data from the Florida
> Department of Health.

The report from the agency indicated that of the 8,995 confirmed cases reported through Aug. 24, 80% or 7,282 cases were discovered among children aged 5 to 17. Before the report, the agency had confirmed that 78.5% of positive cases of the virus were shared among children aged 5 to 17.

As of Monday, Florida had reported 17,311 positive cases for those aged 14 to 17 and 8,248 cases for those aged 11 to 13. A total of 12,946 positive cases were confirmed for those aged 5 to 10 and 7,616 cases for those aged 1 to 4. A total of 2,609 cases were reported among children under 1 year old.

In addition to the increase in COVID-19 cases in children, the state saw hospitalizations rise from 436 to 602 among children as well. Overall, there was one child death, bringing the total death count to eight children in the state.

Leadership in the state hadn't helped. As with the nation's President, Governor DeSantis wanted the state's schools to open but, also like Trump, the courts have other ideas when there's a Constitution in place[68]:

Leon County Circuit Judge Charles Dodson on Monday issued a temporary injunction accusing Gov. Ron DeSantis, Education Commissioner Richard Corcoran and other state education officials of ignoring the Florida Constitution by requiring school districts to resume face-to-face instruction this month amid the coronavirus pandemic.

Attorneys for Corcoran and DeSantis immediately filed a notice of appealing Dodson's ruling to the 1st District Court of Appeal.

Under law, that notice of appeal automatically placed a stay on Dodson's ruling — effectively putting it on hold until the Tallahassee-based appeals court can resolve the case.

Late Tuesday, attorneys for the Florida Education Association and the Orange County teachers union asked Dodson to lift the stay. The following day, the state's lawyers argued the stay should remain in place, saying that failing to do so would "sow confusion and disarray" among students, local school officials and families.

Dodson rejected the state's arguments. Regardless, out-of-control executives were making a political football of schools and children. It showed up in the trenches, at the schools. Adherence to safety protocols were lukewarm.

A sign at Eccleston Elementary School in Florida says masks are recommended, not required[69]. Photo credit: Orange County Classroom Teachers Association/Facebook

The State continued its protracted fight against safe practices in the school re-openings[70]:

On Tuesday, a circuit judge upheld Gadsden
County's mask-wearing mandate and admonished
the challenger's attorney, Anthony Sabatini, a
Republican state lawmaker. "At least four other
courts have rejected challenges to local Florida
mask ordinances that are stated exactly as stated
in the present case. This begs the question, when
is enough enough?" the judge wrote.

All of this is in the context of Florida's positivity rates double the
national average.

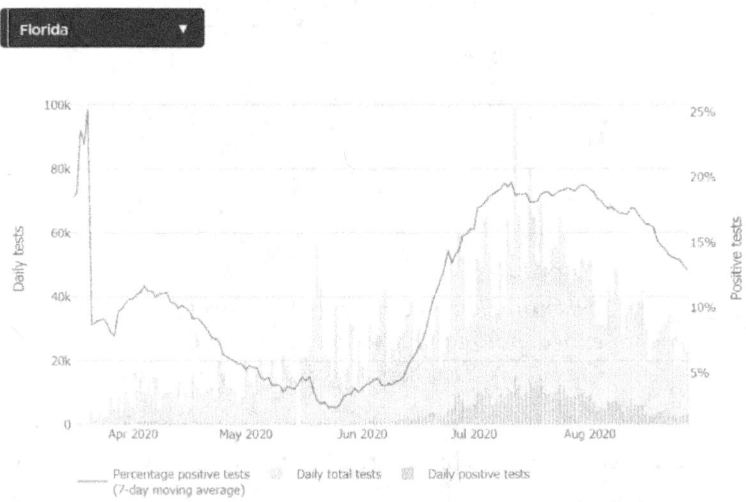

Florida positivity rates at 12.9% as schools in the midst of re-opening. The U.S. rate stands at 5.9%.[71]

University opening were faring poorly as well. The University of Alabama reported that an additional 481 cases had been found on its campuses, bringing that system's total to more than 1,300 since the campuses opened earlier in the month[72]. Only 420 students of the system's over 46,000 students had tested positive before returning to the campus. Those students were not allowed to return.

Meanwhile, denial was in the air. Dr. Scott Atlas, appointee to the coronavirus task force and proponent of herd immunity advocated that children were non-players in the pandemic[73]:

> It was back to school for thousands of Florida students Monday while President Donald Trump's new pandemic adviser dismissed teachers' and parents' COVID-19 concerns as "hysterical" amid reports of a big jump in the number of kids who have tested positive in districts that resumed in-person instruction.

> "We are the only country of our peer nations in the Western world who are this hysterical about opening schools," the adviser, Dr. Scott Atlas, said as he pressed Florida Gov. Ron DeSantis and his advisers to reopen schools as quickly as possible.

Atlas pushed DeSantis on the issue during a roundtable discussion held in Tallahassee on Monday. The number of confirmed cases in Florida climbed over the weekend to 620,000 and the number of deaths eclipsed 11,200, making it one of the hardest-hit states in the country, the latest NBC News figures showed.

Meanwhile, COVID-19 cases in children jumped by more than 23 percent with about 9,200 new infections in the last two-plus weeks, according to news reports citing Florida Department of Health data. Most of the new cases were teenagers between the ages of 14 and 17.

"The recent August numbers represent a whopping 191% increase in children infected in Florida from only about six weeks earlier on July 9," the South Florida Sun-Sentinel newspaper reported.

Atlas, however, insisted the chances of children getting infected are "extraordinarily low." He is a senior fellow at the conservative Hoover Institution at Stanford University and a physician.

So, the U.S. exited August with its children running about in the DMZ to determine whether there were landmines. The ship was headed for the rocks later that year.

A year after the North Paulding High School incident, the scene simply repeated itself. As children returned to schools in the fall of 2021, they were unvaccinated and, with half their parents unvaccinated, the schools became fertile breeding grounds for the virus. The delta variant of the virus ripped through unvaccinated communities in the late summer of 2021, and began to run out of targets in September. However, children were sent into a dangerous situation at the behest of their parents and the schools. A significant number of these children under-18 contracted Covid-19 – approximately 3% of the hospital admissions. In the U.S. at the end of September, 2021, 174 children aged 0-4 had died[74]. Globally, approximately 0.3% of deaths occurred in children and adolescents under 20.[75]

Innocent children unwittingly thrust in harm's way. And this lumped on top of the horrific sexual abuse unveiled in the Catholic Church. How might this square with a good and loving God?

Chapter 4: The Problem of Suffering

Humans are quickly and easily crushed by natural forces, violent or not. Simple changes in temperature can kill them. Predators can quickly end them. Storms can drown. Lightning can fry.

Species down the food chain are even more susceptible, though it is most likely predators that are of greater concern. Violence is the norm; lifespans generally not spanning, but prematurely ending.

In the course of nature, this cycle, this violence is taken for granted. It is what has always been; it is what always will be. Only evolution is the friend, hopefully making the surviving offspring more resilient: better at running, better at hiding, better at flying, better.

In theology, however, it is the problem of suffering: why do innocents suffer? Why is untimely death meted out so randomly? Why, simply by virtue of birth, must suffering and death follow? This problem has tormented theologians and philosophers for thousands of years.

The reverse is: why do the evil prosper? Why might a dictator who tortured and killed thousands die a sudden, drug-induced death without pain? We leave this flip-side question for others to answer: our attention will be on children playing on a beach and salmon, the innocents.

From a theological standpoint, a super-natural power is lurking. A myriad of questions crops up: how many of these powers are there? What do they or it represent? If they have created lesser beings, do they care about the offspring's welfare? Are they awake? Or, are they self-absorbed and cold?

Regarding the lesser beings, are all of interest to the powers? Or, are there creatures that, while feeling obvious pain in their struggle for life, are of no importance to the powers? Do the powers care for the salmon?

Finally, if the powers exist, do we wish them to exist? Are they to be opposed in their cruelty? Avoided? Hated or loved? Tolerated? What is our relationship to them or it? If a bad relationship, what did the salmon do to deserve it?

Polytheism

The earliest religions simply ascribed violent events to violent gods and goddesses, many warring with one another. Gods and goddesses proliferated as required, and just about every object had an associated deity. There was little need for reconciling conflicts within a single entity: there was only warfare between this panoply of forces.

This had some benefit to humans by placing blame on some higher plane. You suffer? Your local goddess is having a bad day. But such a system is anarchic: it provides little understanding to how to control – if possible – these forces. As well, the momentary ascendency of one goddess may, in that moment, impart ascendency to the human group promoting that goddess' star. It is a political nightmare.

In a highly fragmented tribal world, polytheism also allows each tribe its own deity who can bestow good and destroy enemies. Thus, armies do not battle each other under the same god. The opponent is not a heretic, but simply under the protection of another god, possibly weaker, possibly stronger than one's own deity.

Add to this world the human invention of blood sacrifice. Now, clearly, the suffering is by humans and for humans. The more innocent the victim, the more successful the sacrifice is likely to be. Virgins are particularly effective. Not only is suffering a non-concern, the more of it the better.

Dualism

If the pantheon is reduced to a good force versus an evil force, new problems immediately creep in. Why do regular natural events – and so predictable – destroy whomever is in a given locale? This does not seem to be a battle between somewhat balanced powers where sometimes one loses and sometimes one wins. If one power is always the winner, why does the loser hang around? If one power has the upper hand, why not annihilate the opposition?

What is good and what is evil? Is my salmon dinner good? Not for the salmon, surely. Do salmon have the same dual gods? Or, are all gods reserved for humans for whatever reason?

And, returning to the human need for religions that reinforce political power, the game becomes simply one of casting the opposing camp as evil, though this does not guarantee victory on the playing field under the dualism model.

However, this need to cast one's enemies as under the sway of the evil force is powerful in the human political arena. Accordingly, mankind has been slow to reject it; indeed, it has not.

Monotheism

With monotheism, however, the conflicts between good and evil collapse into a single entity, and these require rationalization in order to avoid ascribing multiple personalities to a single entity. Severe psychotherapy is needed.

Job

The story of Job is the heart-wrenching attempt of humans to cope with a God in the time of suffering. It is a discourse that is remarkably unsatisfying at its conclusion. God puffs his chest, and that is the end of it, a not unusual argument. The only solution is to reject any logic whatsoever. Job begins:

> Then Job began to speak and said:
> "Why did I not die at birth,
> Breathe my last when I was born?
> I should then have lain down in quiet,
> Should have slept and been at rest
> With kings and counsellors of earth,
> Who built themselves great pyramids;
> With princes rich in gold,
> Who filled their houses with silver.

The first defense for suffering is that it is only to correct those
on the wrong path:

> Then Eliphaz, the Temanite, answered:
> "If one dares to speak, will it vex you?
> But who can keep from speaking?
> See! you have instructed many,
> And strengthened the drooping hands.
> Your words have upheld the fallen,
> Giving strength to tottering knees.
> But now that trouble comes, you are impatient,
> Now that it touches you, you lose courage.
>
> "Is not your religion your confidence;
> Your blameless life, your hope?
> Remember! What innocent man ever perished?
> Or where were the upright ever destroyed?
> Happy the man whom God corrects;
> Therefore, spurn not the Almighty's chastening.
> For he causes pain but to comfort,
> And wounds, that his hands may heal."

Job replies that he is mortal:

Then Job answered:

"What strength have I, that I should endure?

And what is my future, that I should be patient?

Is my strength the strength of stones,

Or is my body made of brass?

A friend should be kind to one fainting,

Though he lose his faith in the Almighty.

Teach me, and I will keep silent.

Show me how I have sinned."

The next defense is a tautology: God is good because He is good:

Then Bildad, the Shuhite, answered:

"Is God a God of injustice?

Or can the Almighty do wrong?

If your children sinned against him,

He has let them suffer the penalty;

But you should earnestly seek him,

And devoutly beseech the Almighty.

If you are pure and upright,

He will surely answer your prayer,

And will prosper your righteous abode."

Job is not satisfied with that argument:

Therefore, I openly declare:

He destroys the blameless as well as the wicked."

But his friends only repeat the earlier argument:

Then Zophar, the Naamathite, answered:

"If you would cleanse your heart,

And stretch out your hands to God,

And put away sin from your hand,

And let no wrong dwell in your tent,

You would then lift your face without spot,

You would then be steadfast and fearless."

Again, Job defends his behavior, and points out God's erratic

behavior, as if God is actually simple chance:

"Oh, to be as in months of old,

As in days when God guarded my steps,

When his lamp shone above my head,

And I walked by his light through the darkness;

As I was in my prosperous days,

When God protected my tent;

When still the Almighty was with me,

And my children were all about me!

"When I went to the gate of the city,

And took my seat in the open,

The youths, when they saw me, retired,

And the aged rose up and stood;

The princes refrained from talking,

And laid their hands on their mouths;

The voices of nobles were hushed,

And their tongues stuck fast to their palates.

"He who heard of me called me happy,

He who saw me bore me witness,

For I saved the poor who cried,

And the orphan with none to help him.

The suffering gave me their blessing,

And I made the widow's heart glad.

"Eyes was I to the blind,

Feet was I to the lame,

And a father to those who were needy.

I defended the cause of the stranger,

I shattered the jaws of the wicked,

And wrested the prey from his teeth.

"Men listened to me eagerly,
And in silence awaited my counsel.
After my words they spoke not,
And my speech fell as rain-drops upon them.
But they sing of me now in derision,
And my name is a by-word among them.

Exasperated, he challenges God to respond:

"Oh, for some one to hear me!
Behold my defense all signed!
Let now the Almighty answer,
Let Jehovah write the charge!
On my shoulder I would bear it,
As a crown I would bind it round me;
I would tell him my every act;
Like a prince I would enter his presence!"

And, boom! A reply comes, with puffery rather than help:

Then out of the whirlwind Jehovah answered Job:
"Where were you when I founded the earth?

You have knowledge and insight, so tell me.

You must know! Who determined its measures?

Or who measured it off with a line?

On what were its foundations placed?

Or who laid its corner-stone,

When the morning stars all sang together,

And the sons of God shouted for joy?

"Can you lift up your voice to the clouds,

That abundance of water may answer you?

Can you send on their missions the lightnings;

To you do they say, 'Here we are'?

"Does the hawk soar because of your wisdom,

And stretch her wings to the south wind?

Does the eagle mount up at your bidding,

And build her nest on high?

"Will the fault-finder strive with Almighty?

He who argues with God, let him answer.

Will you set aside my judgment,

And condemn me, that you may be justified?"

Then Job answered the Lord:

> "How small I am! what can I answer?
> I lay my hand on my mouth.
> I spoke once, but will do so no more;
> Yes, twice, but will go no further.

This is an ad hominem "I am so big, you are so small" argument, not even approaching an answer to the question, "Why is Job suffering?" But, Job caves in. Not much choice:

> "I know thou canst do all things,
> And that nothing with thee is impossible.
> I spoke, therefore, without sense,
> Of wonders beyond my knowledge.
> I had heard of thee but by hearsay,
> But now my eye has seen thee;
> Therefore I despise my words,
> And repent in dust and ashes."

So, well, the Story of Job is not very helpful. God's argument is simply that, well, He's God, deal with it. That, of course, is nearly in line with evolution and natural selection. The God of Job is not whom we might label as a "caring" God.

And is Job's circumstance really different from that of every other human? Job came from a background of riches and education. He had the luxury of caring for others. But this is not the lot assigned to most of humanity. Job is the exception, yet even that exception does not relieve him of suffering.

St. Augustine

For Augustine, suffering is meted out equally, but the reaction of the sufferer is what matters: "Though the suffering the same...the sufferers remain different."[76] Suffering for the believer is an opportunity, not a problem:

> "Trials and tribulations offer us a chance to make reparation for our past faults and sins. On such occasions the Lord comes to us like a physician to heal the wounds left by our sins. Tribulation is the divine medicine."

This is a massive stretch of logic. It assumes that God has no better teaching mechanism than the paddle, and that the believer owes God something that suffering alone pays.

More problematic: Augustine equates suffering with sin, and forgets about Job and the innocents. They do not play in the equation, and one wonders why.

St. Augustine's logic gets handed down under a category, "Don't Waste Your Suffering", getting ever more twisted as they appear in visions:

> "And the Lord said to me, 'My child, you please Me most by suffering. In your physical as well as your mental sufferings, My daughter, do not seek sympathy from creatures. I want the fragrance of your suffering to be pure and unadulterated. I want you to detach yourself, not only from creatures, but also from yourself...The more you will come to love suffering, My daughter, the purer your love for Me will be.'"[77]

The suffering of the innocents is now a goal. This does nothing to help us believe that this God – who enjoys the suffering – is Good.

Creator-only

If the single deity is a Creator only, and does not care about the follow-on knocks of the creation, then the problem of suffering goes away. This Creator is removed from any personal relationship to humans. Their travails are either of their own devices, or the result of so many ping-pong balls bouncing around in the lottery machine.

The Creator looks more like a physics phenomenon. The Big Bang defines the Creator, who may be busy with innumerable other Big Bangs, having created the Universe simply as one experiment out of many – perhaps a disappointing experiment. No matter, there are other universes.

Mass-extinction events

The story of Job is the story of an individual, and anthrocentric. Job's righteousness – his supposed armor against suffering – is owned by him and is his alone.

What of mass-extinction events, where there is no "out" for any member of a large group? What of tsunamis? What of pandemics?

The God of Job would have an even more difficult time explaining these, except that he's already employed the only reason available: it is what it is. Any difference in "righteousness" within the group is immaterial. It is the group as a whole that suffers. In this case, we are thrust into the Sodom and Gomorrah story, where the behavior of an entire city is uniformly bad, not an exception among their inhabitants. Of course this is impossible! There are certainly newborns and young children who have not made conscious choices that might be considered to have moral content. More likely? Mother Nature was having a bad day.

In fact, life is mass-extinction in slow-motion. Death is the inevitable end, and that end is generally unpleasant except in rare circumstances. It is also the rule of life in an evolutionary system. Death must occur for there to be room for further life. A cycle must exist, else life would not have progressed beyond a single-celled form that overran the world and still overwhelms it.

Food chains

Food chains are simply persistent, on-going mass-fatality events. Why would a Creator, if caring, create a food chain? Why wouldn't photosynthesis be the common denominator of life? Why cannot the energy of the Sun be sufficient for all?

Introducing a food chain multiplies suffering by several times. It makes the possibility of suffering – fear – ever-present. There is little rest.

How might a good power allow this?

In the Judeo-Christian tradition, it was simple: animals don't matter much. Some lip-service may be given, such as Noah and his Ark, but animals were more property than worthy. Or, rather, their worth was in their provision of value to humans. Humans were – and still are – clearly the main show.

In this view, with humans firmly atop the food chain (or, thinking they were), any suffering on down is incidental, even unimportant. That wail of the elephant? Meaningless.

Other traditions hold animals in higher esteem.

Suffering, logic, and Creator

Possibly originating with Greek philosopher Epicurus, the philosopher Hume summarizes Epicurus's version of the problem as follows: "Is God willing to prevent evil, but not able? Then he is not omnipotent. Is he able, but not willing? Then he is malevolent. Is he both able and willing? Then from whence comes evil?" The logical argument from evil is as follows[78]:

> *P1. If an omnipotent, omnibenevolent and omniscient god exists, then evil does not.*

P2. There is evil in the world.

C1. Therefore, an omnipotent, omnibenevolent and omniscient god does not exist.

This argument is of the form modus tollens: If its premise (P1) is true, the conclusion (C1) follows of necessity. To show that the first premise is plausible, subsequent versions tend to expand on it, such as:

P1a. God exists.

P1b. God is omnipotent, omnibenevolent and omniscient.

P1c. An omnipotent being has the power to prevent that evil from coming into existence.

P1d. An omnibenevolent being would want to prevent all evils.

P1e. An omniscient being knows every way in which evils can come into existence, and knows every way in which those evils could be prevented.

P1f. A being who knows every way in which an evil can come into existence, who is able to prevent that

evil from coming into existence, and who wants to do
so, would prevent the existence of that evil.

P1. If there exists an omnipotent, omnibenevolent
and omniscient God, then no evil exists.

P2. Evil exists (logical contradiction).

Both of these arguments are understood to be presenting two forms of the 'logical' problem of evil. They attempt to show that the assumed premises lead to a logical contradiction that cannot all be correct. Most philosophical debate has focused on the suggestion that God would want to prevent all evils and therefore cannot coexist with any evils (premises P1d and P1f), but there are existing responses to every premise (such as Plantinga's response to P1c), with defenders of theism (for example, St. Augustine and Leibniz) arguing that God could exist and allow evil if there were good reasons.

The evidential problem of evil (also referred to as the probabilistic or inductive version of the problem) seeks to show that the existence of evil, although logically consistent with the existence of God, counts against or lowers the probability of the truth of theism. Both absolute versions and relative versions of the evidential problems of evil:[79]

> *There exist instances of intense suffering which an omnipotent, omniscient being could have prevented without thereby losing some greater good or permitting some evil equally bad or worse.*

> *An omniscient, wholly good being would prevent the occurrence of any intense suffering it could, unless it could not do so without thereby losing some greater good or permitting some evil equally bad or worse.*

> *(Therefore) There does not exist an omnipotent, omniscient, wholly good being.*

The problem of evil has also been extended beyond human suffering, to include suffering of animals from cruelty, disease and evil. One version of this problem includes animal suffering from natural evil, such as the violence and fear faced by animals from predators, natural disasters, over the history of evolution. This is also referred to as the Darwinian problem of evil, after Charles Darwin who wrote in 1856 "What a book a Devil's chaplain might write on the clumsy, wasteful, blundering low & horridly cruel works of nature!", and in his later autobiography said "A being so powerful and so full of knowledge as a God who could create the universe, is to our finite minds omnipotent and omniscient, and it revolts our understanding to suppose that his benevolence is not unbounded, for what advantage can there be in the sufferings of millions of the lower animals throughout almost endless time? This very old argument from the existence of suffering against the existence of an intelligent first cause seems to me a strong one".

The second version of the problem of evil applied to animals, and avoidable suffering experienced by them, is one caused by some human beings, such as from animal cruelty or when they are shot or slaughtered. This version of the problem of evil has been used by scholars including John Hick to counter the responses and defenses to the problem of evil such as suffering being a means to perfect the morals and greater good because animals are innocent, helpless, amoral but sentient victims. Scholar Michael Almeida said this was "perhaps the most serious and difficult" version of the problem of evil. The problem of evil in the context of animal suffering, states Almeida, can be stated as:

P1 God is omnipotent, omniscient and wholly good.

P2 The evil of extensive animal suffering exists.

> *P3 Necessarily, God can actualize an evolutionary perfect world.*

> *P4 Necessarily, God can actualize an evolutionary perfect world only if God does actualize an evolutionary perfect world.*

> *P5 Necessarily, God actualized an evolutionary perfect world.*

If #1 is true then either #2 or #5 is true, but not both. This is a contradiction, so #1 is not true.

Defenses

Various defenses are offered for the logical inconsistency of a good Creator with the massive suffering in front of us.

Where reason ends, faith begins

This begs the questions: Does reason end? Does it have a start and finish? Is it time constrained? Why must it end? If an argument reaches its logical conclusion, does reason end, or simply suspend?

If one moves beyond reason, one must necessarily reject it if the new beliefs contradict it.

Leap of faith

This would seem to be more of an escape. Why is the leap required? What is requiring it? When the leap is made, what happens to reason which was likely the jumping off point? What happens to the brain?

Choice between evolution and two-faced Creator

In a monotheistic system dominated in the natural world by food chains, the choice boils down to the following:

1] The Creator has put in place a system for perpetual gladiatorial combat between all species, regardless of what they do, *or*

2] Life competes fiercely in a deadly battle for scarce resources.

So, quite evil Creator, or no Creator. There is no other option, given food chains.

This is problematic for the Judeo-Christian tradition, and others that attempt to explain away suffering as necessary to something other than providing a predator something.

Tsunamis wash over the land, destroying all in their path. Salmon are consigned to 4-year migration leaving 1 out of 5,000 alive at the end. Children are sent to their death by their parents.

One work-around is to 1] consider plants and animals the unlucky parts of a food chain that serves humans and of no concern to the Creator, and 2] allocate "true suffering" to humans alone, despite the observation of grief in other species. That is cold, very cold. It is chilling in its callousness. Yet, it is the Devil's Bargain that believers in a Good Creator must accept. But, regardless, it is also a cumbersome work-around, forcing the believer to psychoanalyze the Creator.

The cognitive dissonance resulting from believing in a Good Creator in a time of heightened suffering – such as 9/11 – perhaps leads to anger toward, even denial of, the Creator.

Why humans need good and evil

Notions of good and evil help to organize humans, providing first-order principles to keep them from constantly warring on each other. There is no necessity that these concepts exist in fact, they can be and are constructs upon which humans build religious and legal systems.

It is far easier to maintain order with the threat of punishment and the promise of reward for certain behavior. As a belief in an omniscient Enforcer permeates a group, that group starts to self-manage the behavior of its members.

But, again, the thing known as "Good" need only be accepted, real or not.

Occam's razor

In the 4th century B.C., Aristotle wrote in his Posterior Analytics: "We may assume the superiority *ceteris paribus* [other things being equal] of the demonstration which derives from fewer postulates or hypotheses." Today, this is a powerful principle in medicine, known as Occam's razor: in uncertainty, the simplest explanation is likely the best. The term razor refers to distinguishing between two hypotheses either by "shaving away" unnecessary assumptions or cutting apart two similar conclusions.[80]

Put another way: don't create a complex explanation with many ifs and buts when a simple explanation is available.

This makes quick work of the complex defenses put forth for a good Creator in a ruthless world.

Chapter 5: So what?

Why this ending to the stories of the ghost forests, salmon, and viruses? Perhaps it is because humans tend to place themselves in a special category of life, somehow beyond the rules of the rest of life. We cling to the notion of a good Creator who will forgive us when we know full well we must simply never start what we are doing to our environment and the life on it. If we could only see the suffering around us clearly, it would be easier to stop.

Is there suffering? Yes. Is it meaningful, special to you? No. Suffering is the universal state that life takes when it is imperiled. It may be physical suffering, it may be mental, it may even be imaginary, simply fear.

A Creator that is only good cannot be a part of it. This would make it meaningful only to humans, and exclude salmon. Indeed, all non-human life would therefore be outside the dominion of such a supposedly "good" Creator.

This Good God we speak of, then, is simply a reflection of us. We can embrace that. But this must be a God of all, not the God of me. To pray for my relief and not recognize the enormity of suffering all around is not only selfish, it is sad. If this God inflicts pain on our enemies, it is because we wish it so. If this

God comes to the aid of our neighbor, it is because we are not simply the agent of that help, we have willed it.

If we can wiggle free from the attractive but ultimately illusory vision of a good Creator who cares about us as a miraculous and single human, we can move on to a better and truer understanding of our place in this fragile world, beset with anguish and, ultimately, death.

We might, instead, accept a view of life as partners in a finite world where suffering abounds, our duty being to minimize it for all creatures as we are able. Embrace the natural world. Protect it. Nurture it.

What you have in life is those fellow salmon swimming upstream with you. That's it.

149

Appendices

Appendix A: Getting there

Ghost Forest

The Copalis ghost forest is located near Copalis Beach on Washington's Pacific coast. Out of Aberdeen, follow US-101 north, then head west on SR-109.

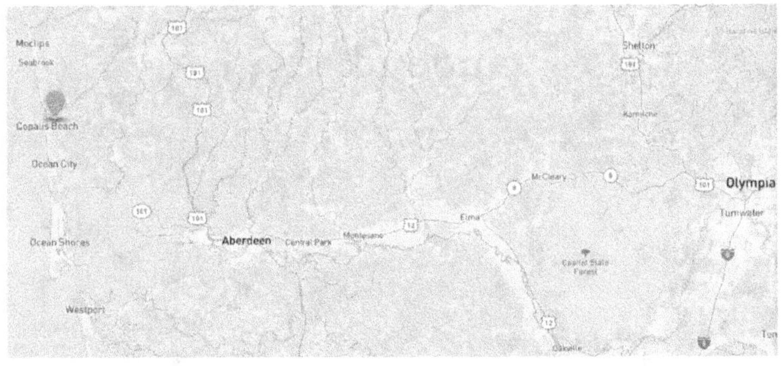

Copalis Beach is due west from Olympia on the Pacific Ocean. USGS Topoview

In Copalis Beach, the Green Lantern Pub is on the west side of SR-109. Park in the lot across the street overlooking the river. There's an informal path leading to the river that will allow you to launch your kayak or paddleboard. Be sure to time the tides.

It'll be easier to head upriver with the tide coming in, then reverse course as it heads out again. However, not as many of the stumps are visible at high tide.

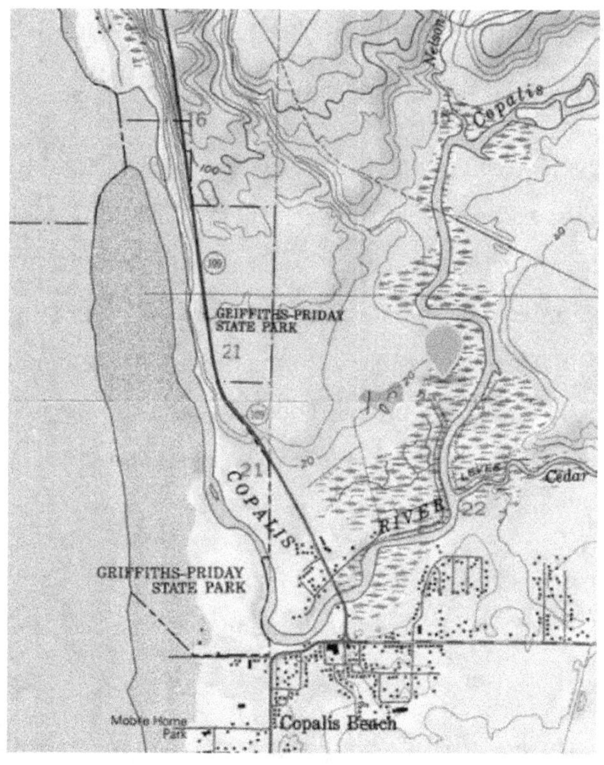

The ghost forest is located a few hundred yards upstream on the Copalis River. USGS topoView.

Elwah River

The Elwah River meets the Straits of Juan de Fuca a mile west of Port Angeles on the Olympic Peninsula's northern coast.

Traveling west on US-101 out of Port Angeles, take a right on SR-112. The Lower Dam Road is a quarter mile ahead on your left.

Quinault River

All access to the Quinault River between the ocean and Lake Quinault must be done through the Quinault Nation. However, the river can be reached above Lake Quinault. Take US-101 north out of Aberdeen for 47 miles and turn right on South Shore Drive. The lake is accessible from the campgrounds along the shore as well as Lake Quinault Lodge. Another couple miles up the road and the river comes into view. There are several pull-offs where you can reach the river bank.

If day hiking is in the cards, a hike up the river from Graves Creek campground to Pony Bridge lands you at a beautiful gorge carved by the river.

For backpackers, an easy 13 mile trail takes you to Enchanted Valley with a view of Anderson Glacier, the source of the Quinault River.

Moving day at Quinault National Fish Hatchery

Quinault National Fish Hatchery

Travelling US-101 north of Aberdeen, head west on S-26 (Moclips Highway) for 5 miles. The hatchery is on the north side of the road.

Fish are released from the hatchery into Cook Creek which flows in the Quinault River.

Washington State Humptulips Hatchery

About ten miles from the Quinault National Fish Hatchery is the Washington State counterpart which releases its fish into the Humptulips River.

From US-101 north of Aberdeen, head west on Kirkpatrick Road at the town of Humptulips. The hatchery is on the south side of the road.

For sport fishers with licenses, there are several access points to the Humptulips River along Kirkpatrick Road.

Humptulips River

BucksNW

Located in Seabrook and Pacific Beach off SR-109, BucksNW provides guides and equipment for most activities on and near the coast.

http://www.bucksnw.com

Seabrook

Arrangements can also be made through the concierge at Seabrook Cottage Rentals in Seabrook. Homes varying in size from one to six bedrooms can be rented year-round. BucksNW has a shop here as well.

http://www.seabrookwa.com

Seabrook

Iron Springs Resort.

Iron Springs Resort

The resort is a couple miles north of Copalis Beach on SR-109. Its cabins have spectacular views of the Pacific. Nothing quite like waking up in the down comforters with a storm brewing in the west.

Eats: In addition to the restaurants in Seabrook, Check out the Green Lantern Pub just a few miles south on 109. The pub has a great Caesar Salad with Salmon.

Lake Quinault Lodge with lawn leading to water's edge.

Lake Quinault

Take US-101 north out of Hoquiam. There are exactly 13 road signs as you approach South Shore Drive. Follow any of the 13.

Eats: The Quinault Lodge's breakfasts are superb. From the dining room you can watch colorful male hummingbirds contend for about six feeders outside the windows. The females have no problems.

Just a mile further east on South Shore Drive is the Salmon House, easily the best salmon dinners on the peninsula. Choose from baked, Cajun, or pepper jelly, and don't forget the cheese garlic bread.

The Lodge was built in under a year during the early 1930s. Its lobby is expansive and welcoming.

North Shore

If you're looking for an extended stay, also consider Lochaerie Resort on North Shore Drive. More rustic than the Lodge, the Resort has 6 cabins with tremendous views of the entire

Lake Quinault Lodge

Lake and eastward up the Quinault River toward Mt. Anderson. The Resort opened in 1926, the same year as the Lodge. Call ahead to make sure your dog will be allowed.

Cabin at Lochaerie Resort on Lake Quinault

Appendix B: Great salmon dinners

To appreciate the bounty of the salmon's gift to us, visit some of the great restaurants on the Olympic peninsula. Here are a few worth a visit or two:

Salmon House, Lake Quinault

By far and away the author's favorite, the baked and blackened dinners from the Salmon House are not rivaled. What's better? Enjoy this all on the lawn facing westward toward the lake and the low mountains beyond. Evening could not be better.

Diet notwithstanding, consider adding the cheesy garlic bread as a side, and try not to spoil your dinner.

Green Lantern Pub, Copalis Beach

As somewhat of a dark-horse contender, there's the Green Lantern Pub in Copalis Beach. Order the Caesar Salad with Salmon, and a beautifully cooked and sizable portion of salmon will arrive before you.

Lawn outside the Salmon House.

Appendix C: Footnotes

---

[1] https://quimpergeology.org/2021/atwater-brian/

[2] https://en.wikipedia.org/wiki/1700_Cascadia_earthquake

[3] The tectonic plate theory identifies three forces likely at work: the convection of the mantle, the gravitational push at high ridges, and sinking of the cooling crust.

[4] https://www.nsnews.com/local-news/smaller-earthquakes-pose-greater-risk-than-the-next-big-one-3059921 John Clague, Department of Earth Sciences, Simon Fraser University, British Columbia, speaking at the Parkgate branch of the North Vancouver District Library on October 11, 2017. "In the 1990s Japanese scientists, including Kenji Satake of the Geological Survey of Japan, were tipped off to look back in the historical records after learning of the work of geologist Brian Atwater, dendrochronologist David Yamaguchi and other researchers associated with the University of Washington. They determined through analysis of soil deposits in ancient marshes in estuaries on the Washington state coastline that a cataclysmic earthquake had occurred in the not too distant past. Meticulous Japanese tsunami records not only concurred with that finding, they also narrowed it down to the day and hour that the ocean wave struck their coastline."

Gathering evidence from both the trees and the ground, Atwater determined that the earthquake and tsunami had occurred sometime between 1680 and 1720, but he could not pinpoint the exact date. Japanese scientists, who had extensive records of tsunamis dating back to 684 A.D., read the report, and told Atwater they knew the date, and even the precise time: January 26, 1700, 9:00 P.M. Several hours after the earthquake, tsunami waves had crossed the ocean, and wiped out a fishing village. The Japanese were baffled, because there was no earthquake anywhere near Japan to account for the tsunami. The ghost forest in Washington thus provided the evidence for its origin.

Carbon dating the final growth ring of the trees in the Copalis ghost forest dated the trees last growth to 1699, the year before the tsunami.

5 https://www.livescience.com/3990-orphan-tsunami-frightening-parent.html

6

https://en.wikipedia.org/wiki/2004_Indian_Ocean_earthquake_and_ts unami

7 https://en.wikipedia.org/wiki/1700_Cascadia_earthquake

8 Oregon State University. "Odds are about 1-in-3 that mega-earthquake will hit Pacific Northwest in next 50 years, scientists say." ScienceDaily. ScienceDaily, 25 May 2010. www.sciencedaily.com/releases/2010/05/100524121250.htm

9 https://www.dnr.wa.gov/programs-and-services/geology/geologic-hazards/geologic-hazard-maps#tsunami-inundation

10 "The Really Big One" by Kathryn Schulz, The New Yorker, July 20, 2015

11 https://stonerosefossil.org/

12 https://en.wikipedia.org/wiki/Salmon

13

https://www.science20.com/heidi_henderson/pleistocene_fossil_salmo n_from_the_olympic_peninsula-244198 Pleistocene, a time when the northern part of North America was undergoing a series of glacial advances and retreats that carved their distinctive signature into the Pacific Northwest. It looks as though this population diverged from the original species about one million years ago, possibly when the salmon were deposited at the head of a proglacial lake impounded by the Salmon Springs advancement of a great glacier known as the Puget lobe of the Cordilleran Ice Sheet. Around 17,000 years ago, this 3,000 foot-thick hunk of glacial ice had made its way down from Canada, sculpting a path south and pushing its way between the Cascade and Olympic Mountains. The ice touched down as far south as Olympia, stilled for a few hundred years, then began to melt.

After the ice began melting and retreating north, the landscape slowly changed — both the land and sea levels rising — and great freshwater lakes forming in the lowlands filled with glacial waters from the melting ice. The sea levels rose quite considerably, about one and a half centimetres per year between 18,000 and 13,000 years ago. The isostatic rebound (rising) of the land rose even higher with an elevation gain of about ten centimetres per year from 16,000 to 12,500 years ago.

Around 14,900 years ago, sea-levels had risen to a point where the salty waters of Puget Sound began to slowly fill the lowlands. Both the land and sea continued to rise and by 5,000 years ago, the sea level was about just over 3 meters lower than it is today. The years following were an interesting time in the geologic history of the Pacific Northwest. The geology of the South Fork Skokomish River continued to shift, undergoing a complicated series of glacial damming and river diversions after these salmon remains were deposited.

Today, we find their remains near the head of a former glacial lake at an elevation of 115 metres on land owned by the Green Diamond Company. The first fossil specimens were found back in 2001 by locals fishing for trout along the South Fork Skokomish River.

[14] Idem.

[15] Idem.

[16] https://www.nationalgeographic.org/encyclopedia/photosynthesis/

[17] https://en.wikipedia.org/wiki/Phytoplankton

[18] https://en.wikipedia.org/wiki/Plankton

[19]
https://www.fws.gov/refuge/togiak/wildlife_and_habitat/fish/salmon_li fecycle.html

[20] Idem.

[21] https://e360.yale.edu/features/on-the-northwests-snake-river-the-case-for-dam-removal-grows#:~:text=North%20America%E2%80%99s%20largest%20Pacific%20watershed%2C%20the%20Columbia%20River,tributary%2C%20the%

20Snake%20River%20%E2%80%94%20is%20gaining%20traction Orcas off the coast of Washington are dying of starvation, the direct result of the near-absence of chinook salmon, the foundation of their diet. A whale mother that seemed to mourn her lost calf by carrying its carcass on her back for 17 days as she swam hundreds of miles drew so much international attention that a Seattle Times headline cited "the grief felt around the world."☐ Biologists have observed orcas with "peanut head," ☐a misshapen head and neck brought on by starvation. The three local orca pods are down to 73 animals, from a recent peak of 99 in the late 1980s☐. Given a dearth of reproducing females and a paucity of recent births, the biologists fear that their population has dropped below a sustainable level.

The orcas' plight has refocused attention on the Snake River dams, for their removal offers the most likely prospect of generating chinook — and, in turn, orca — recovery. Even with its dams, the Snake River watershed supports 70 percent of the habitat available for chinook in the entire Columbia Basin — no other dam removals in the Columbia Basin would open as much habitat.

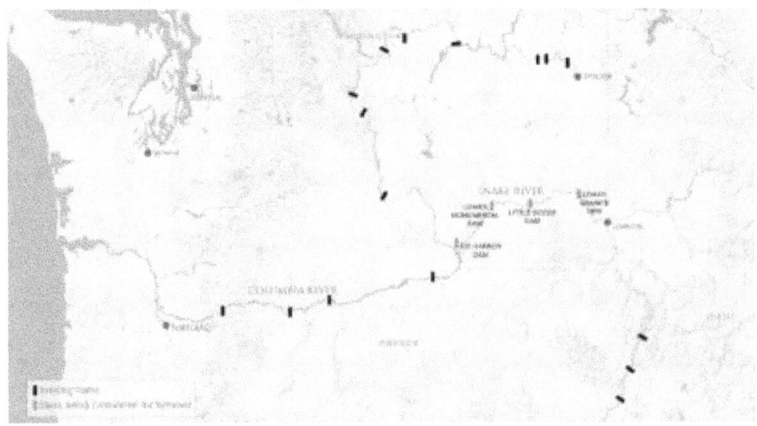

---

[22] https://en.wikipedia.org/wiki/Elwha_River

[23] https://orionmagazine.org/article/a-river-reawakened/

24 https://goia.wa.gov/resources/treaties/quinault-treaty-1856

25 http://www.alaskafishradio.com/inseason-salmon-prices-are-tough-to-track/

26 https://www.thefishsociety.co.uk/fishopedia/salmon-pacific

27 https://www.fws.gov/quinaultnfh/Species.cfm

28 https://www.doi.gov/subsistence/news/general/2021-yukon-river-salmon-fall-fishery-announcement-21-fall-update-9-yukon

29 http://www.adfg.alaska.gov/index.cfm?adfg=hottopics.lowchinookruns_info

30 https://apnews.com/article/climate-change-science-lifestyle-business-environment-and-nature-cb0c966f43e52fd9559857969f1203a0

31 http://www.adfg.alaska.gov/index.cfm?adfg=hottopics.lowchinookruns_info

32 Deer and cars do not mix. Deer are indiscriminately killed by drivers, with 1.5 million accidents in the U.S. each year. https://healthresearchfunding.org/21-significant-deer-car-accidents-statistics/ Of most concern to humans is the damage to their cars. The fate and anguish of the deer is not often considered.

33 Copper engraving of Doctor Schnabel [i.e Dr. Beak], a plague doctor in seventeenth-century Rome, with a satirical macaronic poem ('Vos Creditis, als eine Fabel, / quod scribitur vom Doctor Schnabel') in octosyllabic rhyming couplets. Public domain. Die Karikatur und Satire in der Medizin: Medico-Kunsthistorische Studie von Professor Dr. Eugen Holländer, 2nd edn (Stuttgart:Ferdinand Enke, 1921), fig. 79 (p. 171)

34 https://www.genome.gov/genetics-glossary/Virus

35 https://en.wikipedia.org/wiki/Smallpox

36 Idem.

---

[37] Swan, James Gilchrest, <u>The Northwest Coast, Or Three Years Residence in the Washington Territory</u>, (Sampson, Low, and Son, 1857) pgs. 68 ff.

[38] https://nephrology.wustl.edu/working-together-to-tackle-coronavirus-disease-covid-19/

[39] Huck, Mark, <u>Darkest Winter: Journal of a Pandemic</u> (Amazon, 2021) pg. 40.

[40] Ibid., pg. 352.

[41] Ibid., pg. 492.

[42] https://www.nytimes.com/interactive/2021/us/covid-cases.html. Data taken on October 4, 2021.

[43] Idem.

[44] https://data.mansfieldnewsjournal.com/covid-19-hospital-capacity/facility/grays-harbor-community-hospital/500031/

| Date | All hospital beds | 7 Day Avg. of Bed Occupancy | | | | 7 Day Avg. of Hospitalized COVID-19 Patients | | 7 Day Sum of COVID-19 Admission | | 7 Day Sum of Emergency Department Visit | |
		Adult inpatient beds		ICU Beds		Adult	Pediatric	Adult	Pediatric	COVID-19 Confirmed	Total
Sept. 17, 2021	57.4	99.7%	36.3 of 36.4 beds used	100.0%	4.6 of 4.6 beds used	8.0	N/A	N/A	N/A	49	315
Sept. 10, 2021	62.7	100.0%	42.1 of 42.1 beds used	100.0%	5.6 of 5.6 beds used	10.7	N/A	9	N/A	88	375
Sept. 3, 2021	62.8	97.6%	40.8 of 41.8 beds used	100.0%	6.4 of 9.4 beds used	10.6	N/A	10	N/A	48	267
Aug. 27, 2021	59.7	98.2%	36.0 of 36.7 beds used	86.8%	4.6 of 5.3 beds used	7.0	N/A	5	N/A	35	335
Aug. 20, 2021	54.4	99.3%	43.1 of 43.4 beds used	94.4%	5.1 of 5.4 beds used	7.0	N/A	N/A	N/A	42	301
Aug. 13, 2021	60.9	95.2%	38.0 of 39.9 beds used		N/A	5.9	N/A	N/A	N/A	32	406
Aug. 6, 2021	83.0	92.1%	38.7 of 42.0 beds used		N/A	4.0	N/A	5	N/A	67	421
July 30, 2021	63.3	99.3%	42.0 of 42.3 beds used		N/A	N/A	N/A	N/A	N/A	85	425
July 23, 2021	60.2	93.9%	36.8 of 39.2 beds used	78.8%	6.2 of 6.6 beds used	N/A	N/A	N/A	N/A	45	303
July 16, 2021	60.0	87.2%	34.5 of 39.0 beds used	74.6%	4.4 of 5.9 beds used	N/A	N/A	N/A	N/A	80	392

[45] http://www.healthdata.org/special-analysis/estimation-excess-mortality-due-covid-19-and-scalars-reported-covid-19-deaths

46 Huck, op.cit., pg. 13.

47 https://en.wikipedia.org/wiki/Foot-and-mouth_disease

48 https://www.cdc.gov/mmwr/volumes/69/wr/mm6931e1.htm?s_cid=mm6931e1_w

49 https://www.msn.com/en-us/news/us/9-students-staff-test-positive-for-covid-19-after-georgia-school-hallway-photo-goes-viral/ar-BB17MHNb?ocid=Peregrine

50 https://www.wsj.com/articles/latest-research-points-to-children-carrying-transmitting-coronavirus-11596978001

51 https://www.wsj.com/articles/school-closures-damage-the-youngest-children-11596825976

52 https://www.ajc.com/education/9-cases-of-covid-19-reported-at-north-paulding-high-school/OWH6MN7DZ5A2XDQMXX337AQEWI/

53 https://www.ncbi.nlm.nih.gov/pmc/articles/PMC2862335/

54 Idem.

55 Idem.

56 Huck, op.cit., pg 263.

57 Idem.

58 https://www.msn.com/en-us/news/us/coronavirus-updates-big-12-announces-fall-football-as-other-conferences-postpone/

59 https://twitter.com/GAFollowers/status/1290437298685968385

60 https://www.nytimes.com/2020/08/12/us/georgia-school-coronavirus.html

61 https://www.thedailybeast.com/these-counties-are-feeling-the-heat-from-desantis-to-reopen-schools

62 https://www.ajc.com/education/weekly-covid-19-count-nearly-triples-in-cherokee-county-schools/XYXNYDB4ZZGXTDT5Y7ASYCNNPA/

63 https://www.ajc.com/news/how-white-house-virus-recommendations-square-with-georgias-policies/LE6YJR4UZBBWBM3O5NKMI4AH6U/

64 https://www.azcentral.com/story/news/education/2020/08/14/jo-combs-unified-school-district-not-reopen-teachers/5586523002/

65
https://twitter.com/EricMillerFink/status/1286084419086725121?ref_src=twsrc%5Etfw%7Ctwcamp%5Etweetembed%7Ctwterm%5E1286084419086725121%7Ctwgr%5E&ref_url=https%3A%2F%2Fkvoa.com%2Fnews%2F2020%2F07%2F22%2FEFBBBFteachers-parents-with-clear-message-gather-for-motor-march-as-they-wait-for-more-guidance-on-schools%2F

66 https://www.nytimes.com/2020/08/24/world/covid-19-coronavirus.html?ocid=uxbndlbing#link-bd84ee2

67 https://www.ibtimes.com/florida-sees-nearly-9000-new-covid-19-cases-among-children-schools-reopen-3035168

68 https://www.sun-sentinel.com/coronavirus/fl-ne-schools-ruling-20200827-ihc7i6i6wvdx7dzsuzzviolpxm-story.html

69 https://www.orlandoweekly.com/Blogs/archives/2020/08/05/battle-between-state-and-floridas-largest-teachers-union-intensifies-as-school-openings-near

70 https://www.msn.com/en-us/news/crime/setbacks-for-desantis-lawmaker-on-school-openings-masks/ar-BB18tHeH

71 https://coronavirus.jhu.edu/testing/individual-states/florida Screen capture on 8/28/2020.

72 https://uasystem.edu/covid-19-dashboard/ as reported on 8/28/2020.

73 https://www.nbcnews.com/news/us-news/florida-students-head-back-class-amid-pandemic-reports-more-kids-n1238888

74 https://data.cdc.gov/NCHS/Provisional-COVID-19-Deaths-Focus-on-Ages-0-18-Yea/nr4s-juj3

75 https://data.unicef.org/topic/child-survival/covid-19/

76 Augustine, City of God, Book I, Chapter 8

77 Diary of Saint Maria Faustina Kowalska: Divine Mercy in My Soul

78 https://en.wikipedia.org/wiki/Problem_of_evil

79 Idem.

80 https://en.wikipedia.org/wiki/Occam%27s_razor The phrase Occam's razor did not appear until a few centuries after William of Ockham's death in 1347. Libert Froidmont, in his On Christian Philosophy of the Soul, takes credit for the phrase, speaking of "novacula occami". Ockham did not invent this principle, but the "razor"—and its association with him—may be due to the frequency and effectiveness with which he used it. Ockham stated the principle in various ways, but the most popular version, "Entities are not to be multiplied without necessity" (*Non sunt multiplicanda entia sine necessitate*) was formulated by the Irish Franciscan philosopher John Punch in his 1639 commentary on the works of Duns Scotus.